INSIDE THE
SMALL CHURCH

Anthony G. Pappas
EDITOR

An Alban Institute Publication

Scriptural quotations, unless otherwise noted, are from the New Revised Standard Version of the Bible, copyright © 1989, Division of Christian Education of the National Council of the Churches of Christ in the United States of America, and are used by permission.

Chapters 2, 3, 8, 9, 10, 12, 13, 19, 20, and 29 originally appeared in slightly different forms in *Action Information* and *Congregations: The Alban Journal.* Original copyrights © 1983, 1988, 1990, 1991, 1992, 1993, 1994, and 1998 by the Alban Institute.

Chapters 1, 4, 5, 7, 11, 14, 15, 16, 17, 18, 21, 22, 23, 24, 25, 26, 27, 28, and 30 previously appeared in slightly different forms in *The Five Stones.* Used by permission.

Chapter 6 originally appeared in a slightly different form in *Leaven*, a publication of The National Network of Episcopal Clergy Associations. Used by permission.

Library of Congress Catalog Card Number 2001094866

ISBN 1-56699-251-6

CONTENTS

Anthony G. Pappas

"Who are you?" said the Caterpillar...
"I—I hardly know, Sir, just at present," Alice replied rather
shyly, "at least I know who I was when I got up this morning,
but I think I must have been changed several times since then."[1]

Members of small churches feel an awful lot like Alice. We thought we knew who we were, what church was, how the world operated. We thought we did. But things have changed several times since then. Even when we retreat inside the small church (not all of our being inside the small church is retreat, but it sometimes can be), we find that the small-church world, which we loved and in which we felt so at home, has itself changed several times—or, at least, in several ways. This book is an invitation to healthy and faithful and fruitful functioning inside the small-church world. So it may behoove us to get a handle on some of these shifts.

SIX SIGNIFICANT SHIFTS

Shift #1: Small churches will occupy an increasing proportion of the ecclesiastical landscape.

Small churches have been around a long time. Many would trace their origin all the way back to the upper room experience described in John 20 (although the story of 11 men cowering behind closed doors may not be a birth narrative many of us would want to claim!). Yet certainly the early church was comprised entirely of congregations small enough to meet in homes, probably no more than 30 persons in each.[2] Somehow these little gatherings not only kept the faith, but grew it until Christianity displaced paganism as the religion of the Roman Empire!

Small churches have been at the center of more recent revivals in the church of Jesus Christ too. The impact of class meetings—small, usually home, gatherings for edification and sanctification—on the spread of Methodism comes quickly to mind. Though the roster of specific small churches is constantly changing, their volume is virtually constant—in the United States it appears that a new small church is born for everyone that dies![3]

Despite this historic reality, the future of the small church is the subject of varied opinions. Church consultant Bill Easum claims that up to 75% of existing small churches will be closed before a half-century goes by.[4] Kennon Callahan, another expert on congregational life, asserts that the small church will be one of four viable forms of the church into the foreseeable future.[5] Some would say that two forms of the church will emerge as primary and normative in the days ahead: (1) Large churches that, through the quality and quantity of programming, can meet the expectations of a consumer society; and (2) small churches that can provide the personal touch and warmth so needed as an antidote to our increasingly impersonal culture.

Indeed, 16,000 house churches have come into being in the last few years![6] These are small groups functioning as congregations. They have arrived on the scene almost entirely independently and spontaneously. Collectively, they represent 5% of congregations in the United States! While these are not the typical, mainline small church complete with building, by-laws, and tradition, their emergence bespeaks the soul's need for face-to-face spiritual experience.

And there are more reasons why there will be more small churches in the days ahead. Three congregational realities are converging at the small church. First, *many current midsized churches will become small churches.* Midsized churches are not able to tread water. They are under increasing pressures to maintain their former scale. But they suffer from numerous challenges to doing just that: a diminishment of energy (for instance, single-parent and two-working-parent families); a lessening match with society's interests (that is, lowered social reward for church participation and shifts in taste and style over the generations); an inappropriate administrative system (chaos-controlling rather than permission-giving); the ravages of internal conflict; a pastoral pool that has been filtered and trained for continuity skills rather than innovation skills; and increasing competition from the larger church down the road. Under these and other pressures, more and more midsized churches will slip into the small category.

Second, *denominations are putting more and more energy into starting new churches.* The vast majority of these new churches will be small churches. Some will be small congregations by design and intention. Some will be small churches because their expectations to become large will not be met.

Third, denominations are shifting from an administrative response to a redevelopment model in dealing with small churches. Only a generation ago combining two small and geographically close congregations was seen as good stewardship. Now it is known to be impossible! (That is, the resulting church tends to be, in time, only as strong as the stronger congregation of the original two.) Denominational resources are much more likely now to go into helping waning congregations live into a new and stronger future.[7] The results of these three dynamics will be an increasing proportion of small churches. For good reasons (and for not-so-good reasons as well!), small churches are becoming an increasing part of the landscape.

Shift #2: Small churches will increasingly be recognized as a legitimate form of Christ's body.

For almost the entire 1,900 years after Pentecost, congregational size was not a particularly relevant fact. In Europe churches were organized geographically along parish lines. In colonial America, church size was much less important than congregational maturity and health. The operational question for pastoral placement and satisfaction was, Could a pastor live out his life harmoniously ministering to these folk?[8] But sometime after the Civil War, with a significant increase in immigration, intense and dense urban development, and improved transportation systems,[9] the "large-steeple church" emerged as a new and exciting church form—and small churches have lived in its shadow ever since. (Actually, the source of the shadow has since shifted, first to the large suburban church and then to the megachurch, but the presence of the shadow has been constant!). However, in the 1970s, Carl Dudley gave voice to what most of us knew intuitively, that the small church is a different kind of social entity.[10] To compare it to the large church or megachurch is an apples-to-oranges comparison. The small church was again understood to be a different but equally legitimate social form of Christ's body. Many have written about the family nature of the small church. I have written about its tribal or "people" nature.[11] Increasingly, Christians are able to see size as a dynamic variable rather than as a moral judgment (either way, good or bad!) Christians are increasingly able to disconnect society's value framework from their perceptions of the church (for instance, bigger is not always better, value is not always assessed by quantitative measures, persons are more than means to impersonal ends, and so forth). More and more we are able to say, "Let's assess our churches on their health, faithfulness, and fruitfulness, and not on numerical criteria alone."

Furthermore, pastors are increasingly likely to choose ministry in the small church deliberately—and not as a stepping stone to something bigger but as a legitimate form of soul-satisfying ministry itself! Pastors are starting to identify small-church-appropriate gifts as *being from God!* And some seminaries are offering more specifically small-church training.[12]

Shift #3: Small churches are increasingly understood as more than a simply rural phenomenon and concern.

Of course, the small church was never simply a rural phenomenon. There were always small churches in urban settings—just read the New Testament Epistles! And there often were midsized to even large churches in town settings. But there was a prejudice that said we can grudgingly grant a legitimacy to the small church if we see it as the best that can be done in a sparsely populated area. Yes, there are many places where the only church form possible is a small church. But we now know that the small church is a legitimate congregational form in any demographic setting.

And we are now realizing that the boundaries around the terms *rural* and *urban* have become so fuzzy that it is not always helpful to make a big distinction between them. The computer and the Internet have pushed even further what the automobile, the highway system, and the television had started. Despite geographical separation, because of these technological innovations, we are more like each other than we have ever been. It is now meaningful to talk about one social context in the whole nation despite significant local differences. Setting itself is no longer the best descriptive category. Small churches are everywhere and small-church dynamics operate independent of the setting! So there has been a major shift in congregational analysis *away* from external context and *toward* internal functioning. The "town and country" category for church analysis emphasized setting. The "small church" category emphasizes internal functioning. Furthermore, there is an increasing need for small churches in urban, suburban, and exurban settings. Society is becoming ever more "high tech." Monitor-to-monitor communication is replacing face-to-face relationships. Work is depersonalized. Life has become atomized. In such a world the small church *in any setting* offers the potential for meaningful "high-touch" connections. This is another of the several changes: "small church" has moved away from contextual definition to contentful dynamics.

Shift #4: Small churches are increasingly learning to delight in their faithfulness.

This is true simply because those that don't delight will die! A couple of churches I know have "evangelistic" slogans. These are unspoken, of course, but were they to be articulated, they would announce, "Join our church; our camp needs more bodies for the ongoing church fight," or " Join our church, misery loves company!" P. T. Barnum claimed that there was a sucker born every minute. But very few people will join a church that is sicker (more conflicted, more depressed, more in denial) than they are! Churches that don't live into the joy of the Lord soon won't live at all.

On the other hand, small churches in increasing numbers are learning to be at peace with "smallness." And more than that, they are learning to rejoice and delight in their God-given nature. One of "my" churches (I am an Area Minister with responsibility for 52 American Baptist Churches in southeastern Massachusetts) was in crisis three years ago. This 20-year-old congregation had had been founded with high hopes, but they never seemed to be able to live up to their own and their denominational partners' expectations. Sure, they were doing some things very well. They had a fresh and personal approach to worship. Their space was more homey, less formal, and multifunctional. They were keeping up with their mortgage payments, although just barely. But they were also doing a number of things weakly or not at all. They had slipped back from a full-time pastoral package to part-time. They had abandoned a second worship service when conflict and low attendance conspired to undermine it. They seemed to be stuck in a syndrome of alternating cycles of discouragement and hostility. The crisis came to a head when their pastor was forced to take a medical leave of absence. He and the congregation had tried to live into a definition of success that did not fit them. They had tried to be big and successful and all things to all people and it had darn near killed them both. During his leave the Holy Spirit ministered to the pastor and he developed a more healthy and balanced set of self-expectations. The congregation discovered that they liked being in the theological and stylistic center. They liked both traditional and contemporary music. They upheld the scriptures, but not in a fundamentalistic way. They enjoyed being a "single cell of caring people"[13] rather than a multi-cell, dwarf large church! They had finally given themselves permission to just be themselves. Their pastor came roaring back with joy from ministering as he could, instead of feeling anger and guilt for what he wasn't accomplishing. And for the past two years that church has been a delightful place of joy and peace and love and health!

Shift #5: Small churches will be increasingly variegated in form.

Remember those "good" old days when companies and denominations sought to gain efficiency through standardization? Thank God we have moved on to recognize the uniqueness of every congregation and setting! One shape does not fit all. One form does not work everywhere. There are many factors that intertwine to give shape to ministry in each particular situation. One is the heritage and trajectory of the church. What have we been about lo these many years? What repertory have we developed that will give shape to our future efforts? Another is the congregation's personality and identity. Are we introverted or extraverted? Risk takers or conservatives? Are we ethnic or neighborhood or blue collar? Another is the context. What are the needs around us? What are the opportunities that exist right here, right now? What is God up to in the community? How can we get on board? And we must not forget the partnership potential. What opportunities exist for gaining strength through teaming up?

Two of "my" congregations are exploring a relationship I call "twinning." They are talking about the synergy that could result if they conceived of their two small-church ministries as a team effort. They have determined that the youth ministry of the one could be piggybacked upon by the other. And conversely, the mission effort and commitment of the other would stand as a model and opportunity for involvement by the first! New Testament body-functioning at the congregational level—amazing!

The Episcopalians have pioneered some fresh forms of small church life. Clustering is one. Clusters are groups of two to six small churches that come together to obtain services from a pastoral pool. Each church maintains its own building, events, identity, and so forth. But by pooling pastoral dollars, the cluster is able to have the services of a team of skilled persons! "MOSS" is a second form. The Diocese of Indiana has experimented creating small congregations without buildings or settled priests! Space is obtained by rental or donation, and priestly services are obtained on an itinerant basis. What the diocese discovered is that without the two biggest expenses of a local congregation (plant and pastor), these new churches became mission engines, providing more resources for mission efforts than churches 10 times their size!

The house churches mentioned above are another form of the small congregation. My judicatory is working toward the formation of a deliberately multicultural new congregation. A local church pastor and I are brainstorming how to create an "institution-less" new church whose mission is entirely to equip its members for ministry in their various life settings. And so on and so forth.

The point is: We are coming to see that the God of infinite creativity and variety can shape as many different forms of the small church as we can respond to in obedience. The sky is the limit!

Shift #6: Small churches are increasingly receiving different support from their denominations than in the past.

In the past loyalty, conformity, and uniformity were big values at the denominational level. (I doubt they were ever very big at the local church level!) But now a shift is occurring at the denominational level. We denominational people are coming to realize that two entities are smarter than we are: The first is God, the second is local church folk! The denomination's job is not to push uniformity; rather it is to provide the resources, challenge, processes, and visioning that will catalyze each small church to fulfill its unique divine calling.

So I provide resources when asked that are customized to the request of the congregation. I build networks of God's people with common interests or complementary skills so that they might spark and support each other in growing into their calling. I sense unarticulated needs and invite people to avail themselves of the resources I can place before them. I have given up on guilt as an effective motivator; instead, I try to be constantly hopeful and share our stories of victories and our lessons from failures!

I was astounded when one of my pastors called to tell my he had been "booked" by another of "my" churches to come and defend our denomination in the face of the churches' disgruntlement over some issues. "They felt you would be biased," he explained—and I guess I would be at that! So he and I talked. He went and met with the dissidents. He later reported that he was able to explain a number of points they had misunderstood. He invited them to get involved in a process of constructive change and they concurred that that was the Christian thing to do. And I was miles away! The (denominational family) system has grown to the point where it can effectively handle confrontations internally. Resources flowed to the point of need and solutions were set in place. It isn't heaven yet, but it is movement in the right direction.

Yes, Alice, we have changed several times since morning. But within these changes God is shaping our small churches. Our tools and understandings are growing. Our capacity to discern God's will is being more acute. Our desire to delight in the presence of God in our small congregations is swelling. God is inside the small church. The question is, Can we respond fully to the Divine there?

INSIDE *INSIDE THE SMALL CHURCH*

In the remainder of this volume, we will invite you to respond to the Divine Presence in four ways: through leading, loving, "largening," and leaving the small church.

Part One considers leadership in the small church. Quality leadership in our smaller congregations suffers from being misunderstood and underappreciated. Effective small-church leadership often appears to be quite unremarkable: People visiting other people. Talking. Helping out. Giving room for everyone to express themselves. Making sure all have a role to play. Weaving new people into time honored traditions. Dusting off and trying anew some old activities. Responding to unforeseen events in constructive ways. Trusting God and feeling good and helping others to feel God's goodness. Laughing and crying and praying. Setting boundaries while offering one more chance, again and again. Blowing on embers of hope until they flare up again. Seeing a glimmer of potential and providing a space safe enough to realize it—step by step.

In other words, quality leadership in the small church feels natural, personal, and familial. It is "not jealous or boastful or proud or rude. It does not demand its own way. It is not irritable and keeps no records of wrongs. It delights not in injustice but rejoices in the truth. It never gives up, never loses faith, is always hopeful, and endures most things" (apologies to 1 Corinthians 13!).

Leadership in the small church is easy to miss, to overlook, to think that it is so simple that anyone can do it. The more effective the small-church leader is, the more it seems that there is nothing to it. Yet such leadership is an art. Some do it well, naturally, without a second thought. But it is also a science. This is good news for those of us who need to grow our small-church leadership abilities. The folkways of the small church can be discerned and effective leadership practices can be learned. Part One takes us on a tour of many learnings and discernings.

Doug and Sherry Walrath start us off with a cognitive map of some of the most useful categories for understanding small congregations, pointing to skills and attitudes that help leaders to function effectively in a small-church setting. Richard Griffin helps us to understand that authority in rural and small-town settings is first and foremost sociological. The leader's claim to theological and spiritual authority needs to be understood in light of this pervasive "authority" landscape. Lawrence Farris's discoveries about the role leadership can play in traditional settings are very encouraging. Clay Smith and Gary Farley give us many practical, hands-on tips for moving a small church forward. Steven Norcross and I uplift and examine bivocational ministry. And last, in an article that bridges us into the "loving" section, I argue that, until a pastor can say with Ruth "your people shall be my people," his or her leadership will fall short of "chieftainship."

Part Two dares us to love the small church. It ain't always easy, especially since small churches so rarely love themselves. One cannot breathe the air of our bigger-is-better culture and completely avoid despising small things. Those of us who have found Christ's love and redemption, soul-satisfying relationships, divinely rooted purpose, and God's presence in the context of the small congregation, know that an eternal beauty lives there. In our hearts we may know that small is beautiful, but our heads mock our hearts. We are conflicted about small churches. Can we love the small church as God does and help it to love itself?

If the small church is viewed by its leaders as a stepping stone or a banishment, it will never be truly known or loved. And if the members of small congregations are not accepted simply as God's children (rather than as the means for ministry), they will not be truly known or loved. Learning to love the small congregation—her members (as well as their extended families) and her potential members—is crucial if the small-church leader is to experience satisfaction in ministry and move the small congregation on to greater health.

Loving the small church means, first of all, acceptance. Being at peace that what is in this particular small church *is*. Second, loving the small church means nonacceptance; that is, it is a refusal to see the future of those people with the limitations with which they see themselves. It involves a resolute belief that God has a wondrous future and a joyous adventure in store for them. Third, loving the small church means patience. By its nature, the small church will take a good while to cast off on its joyous adventure, and then will proceed with great caution. And that is OK. Speed is only a human notion.

In Part Two, Steve Burt and Hazel Roper take an objective look at low self-esteem in the small church and offer some constructive ways to build a positive congregational self-image. Loren Mead shares from his experience with small churches eight gifts that such congregations offer to the larger church. Gary Farley takes a clear-headed look at what small churches have going for them and against them. Caroline Westerhoff challenges us to think of the small church as normative, the proper scale of God's creation. Melvin Williams lifts up what can be done *because* a congregation is small. Steve Burt concludes this part with a reminder that "when it comes to doing the work of God—small churches are the right size."

Part Three challenges us to increase the capacity of small congregations to respond in faithfulness to God's call. Often in church literature, in speech, and in thought, the small church is put down, diminished, lessened. Can we instead "largen" the small church? Can we be about the business of enlarging the capacity of the small church to serve God joyfully and productively? God intends to do great things through the quarter-million small congregations in our land! God intends to, but often small churches do not see themselves as players and so take themselves out of the game. In this part we will consider a number of ways to get small churches back in the game!

Clay Smith reminds us that "small-membership churches often have influence and presence in their communities that is all out of proportion to their small size," and he challenges to use that influence and presence! John Koessler helps small-church leaders value particular competencies and let go of "omnicompetence" as a valid small-church goal. Ken Marple looks at the constraints of ministering in rural areas but then goes on to list the advantages and opportunities awaiting faithful, active, and hopeful congregations. Instead of allowing small congregations to wallow in self-pity at their inability to benefit from mass evangelism, Carl Dudley dares us to grow as families do—by birth and adoption. Perry Bell lifts up the role of caring and the primacy of relationships in small congregations as means to growth and stewardship. Small churches are often homogeneous groupings; in his second essay in this section, Ken Marple dares us to love the unlovely, the downtrodden, the broken. I try to demonstrate in my two pieces how small churches can let others in on the love they share. Some do this naturally; most have to learn how. Learning how to share love is not always easy, but it is always necessary. It is this capacity—the capacity to love—that is the hallmark and faithful contribution of the small church.

Leading. Loving. Largening. In Part Four we will consider *leaving* the small church! By "leaving," I do not mean joining a large church. Rather, I mean leaving the "sanctuary" of our small churches to go forth into the world to minister in Christ's name. Often "mission" and "small church" are treated as mutually exclusive realities. The kinds of mission a small church engages in are often qualitatively different from the mission endeavors of larger organizations.[14] Yet small-church ministries can be powerful and pervasive—miraculous, even! Small-church missions are personal, local, rooted, organic, restorative, and responsive. But they do not always register as quantifiable mission. This section has the twofold goal of encouraging small churches to rise to the challenge of ministering to their worlds and of understanding their efforts in categories that are "small-church appropriate."

In Part Four, I start us off with an exploration of mission criteria. John Bennett explores the biblical concept of "remnant" as one model for faithful small-church mission today. David Ray challenges us to organize around local, not denominational, realities! Gary Farley offers two essays in this section; the first invites small churches to discover their unique identity, gifts and calling, and live into it with a passion. The second invites us to realize that our country is not adequately "churched" and pinpoints places where we can give birth to new congregations. Ben Poage delineates six needs that mission efforts must address if small-church mission is to be fresh and powerful. Doug Walrath reminds us that small churches can do social ministry and explores with us the implications. And finally, I invite us to think about some new ways of doing church and mission.

I have lived with many of these articles for some years and in the process have gotten to know many of the authors. Additional articles come from the Alban Institute's long history of concern for small-church health. As Alice noted, the world has changed several times since were first written. But the insights of these foundational essays still hold true. Therefore, I am thrilled to have been invited to edit this volume, and, in turn, to invite you into this family of faithful people who care more for God's call than the world's success. May the contents of this book inform your leadership in your small-church ministry. May God bless you.

NOTES

1. Lewis Carroll, *Alice's Adventures in Wonderland* (New York: Signet Books, 1960), p. 47.

2. Robert Banks, *Paul's Idea of Community: The Early House Churches in Their Historical Setting* (Grand Rapids: Wm. B. Eerdmans, 1980), p. 41.

3. Edward W. Hasinger, John S. Holik, and J. Kenneth Benson, *The Rural Church: Learning from Three Decades of Change* (Nashville: Abingdon Press, 1988), p. 67.

4. Address at "Gathering of Church Champions" Conference, The Leadership Network, Flower Mound, Tx., 1999.

5. Kennon L. Callahan, *A New Beginning for Pastors and Congregations* (San Francisco: Jossey-Bass, 1999), p. 208.

6. Laurie Goodstein, "Search for the Right Church Ends at Home," The *New York Times* (April 29, 2001).

7. See, for example, Alice Mann, *Can Our Church Live? Redeveloping Congregations in Decline* (Bethesda, Md.: The Alban Institute, 1999) and James H. Furr, Mike Bonem, and Jim Herrington, *Leading Congregational Change* (San Francisco: Jossey-Bass, 1999).

8. See Jackson W. Carroll, ed., *Small Churches Are Beautiful* (New York: Harper & Row, 1977).

9. See, for example, "Beecher's Boats," as described in Robert Ellis Smith, *Ben Franklin's Web Site* (Providence, R.I.: The Privacy Journal, 2000), p. 214.

10. Carl Dudley, *Making the Small Church Effective* (Nashville: Abingdon Press, 1978).

11. Anthony G. Pappas, *Entering the World of the Small Church*, revised and expanded edition (Bethesda, Md.: The Alban Institute, 2000).

12. For instance, Bangor Theological Seminary (Maine); Sewanee School of Theology (Tennessee); Dubuque Theological Seminary (Iowa); Pittsburgh Theological Seminary (Pennsylvania); and McMaster University (Ontario, Canada).

13. Dudley, *Making the Small Church Effective*, passim.

14. See my book with Scott Planting, *Mission: The Small Church Reaches Out* (Valley Forge, Penn.: Judson Press, 1993).

Part One
LEADING THE SMALL CHURCH

Chapter 1
SUPPORTING SMALL CONGREGATIONS
AND
THEIR PASTORS

Sherry Walrath and Douglas Alan Walrath

During the latter part of 1986 and early 1987, we conducted intensive research in order to describe the kinds of small churches that dominate our region, and to determine what constitutes "effective" ministry in the various kinds of small congregations found in our region.[1] On the basis of our research, we learned there are different kinds of small churches, and that all those who are concerned with the selection, preparation, placement, and support of pastors in small churches need to understand how these congregations differ from one another. Becoming aware of the different kinds of small churches, particularly during the seminary years, will help pastors and prospective pastors to identify the kinds of small congregations in which they will be able to serve best.

TYPES OF SMALL CHURCHES

In the early 1970s, Doug began to categorize small churches according to the ways they appear to those who live in the areas they serve. He discovered that each gains a reputation in its area. People in an area decide whether they can or want to participate in a church on the basis of the way it appears to them. Listening to pastors in the 1986 survey describe the small churches in our region, we could identify congregations with three kinds of reputations: Dominant, Denominational, and Distinctive.

Dominant Churches

The *Dominant* church is "the" church in its neighborhood or community— the "tall-steepled" church. Local residents usually see it as a moneyed, prestigious church. Often the church building is located on the town square or on a corner lot. Its members expect the best in pastoral leadership and program. People who are regarded as important in the community (or who want to regarded as such) belong to this church. It appears (and most of its members are seen as) socially dominant.

Dominant churches usually thrive when there is an ample supply of relatively affluent, middle-class persons who support what they see as that church's superior leadership, program, and facilities. Wherever such a constituency declines, as it has in many rural communities and small towns, Dominant churches also tend to decline. Economic losses tend to encourage middle-class persons to move elsewhere in search of better job opportunities and thus have a great impact on Dominant churches. Actual losses, however, often do not lead immediately to changed perceptions. Even when they lose their constituency, most Dominant churches do not simultaneously lose their local image. Despite their loss of members and economic support, they are still viewed locally as "the" church. As a result, those remaining in the community who are not the Dominant church's traditional constituency still do not see it as accessible to them.

Many pastors and lay leaders of declining Dominant churches do not seem to appreciate how long a Dominant church continues to be identified with its traditional image—even when it is no longer powerful. They wonder why so few persons in the community respond to their concentrated efforts to welcome them, or to programs developed to meet their needs and interests. Usually such efforts will not bear fruit until those toward whom the efforts are directed are able to change their image of the Dominant church, until they can regard the Dominant church as *their* church. Even people who participate in church programs and benefit from the church's ministry are not able to see themselves as members. They usually do not become regular participants or members until the church gains a new and broader reputation. Often a Dominant church needs to persist for many years in efforts designed to broaden its appeal before others in its area begin to see it as a church in which they can participate.

Denominational Churches

The *Denominational* church is defined locally by the denominational label it carries. People who belong to a Denominational church are identified locally as "Methodists" or "Presbyterians" or "Baptists"—in other words, by the denomination of the local church. Long-standing residents, as well as newcomers who have roots in a given denomination and who continue to function as church members on the basis of those roots, compose the participants of a Denominational church.

Members of small Denominational churches are often very loyal to their church. Those who possess such a strong sense of denominational loyalty maintain their loyalty to a Denominational church even during periods when they are dissatisfied with a particular minister and/or church program. Some members may drop out or withhold their contribution when they are dissatisfied; they may even attend another church for a time. But they rarely withdraw their membership. Their sense of identity both with a congregation and the denomination beyond the local congregation encourages them to wait for a change of pastor or program. When such a change occurs, they usually return.

A Denominational church thrives so long as there is an adequate supply of persons who want to be identified with a congregation connected to the denomination it represents. Like the Dominant church, the Denominational church usually declines when those who compose its traditional supporters move away. In many communities, congregations affiliated with denominations that are seen as middle-class experience increasing difficulty as more and more middle-class persons or their grown children move to metropolitan areas.

The specific reputation, polity, and policies of its denomination help or hinder the local congregation that is clearly identified with a particular denomination. For example, a denomination that can provide uninterrupted pastoral leadership for its small churches through appointments, or that moves quickly to provide solid support for congregations seeking new pastors, may strengthen the position of its congregations.

The position of a Denominational church in the community can also be strengthened or weakened by what local leaders say about their experiences with the denomination, or by what local people see and hear about the denomination in the media. Pastors report local leaders are most frustrated when they are called upon to defend locally unpopular positions their denomination takes on national issues but receive little support or recognition for their efforts to keep their small church going.

Distinctive Churches

The *Distinctive* church is known for one, and occasionally more than one, emphasis. While it may embrace a typical variety of church functions within its life, it is best known locally for that single emphasis. Sometimes people type the Distinctive church according to a theological emphasis ("fundamental," "liberal"). Sometimes its worship style ("charismatic") sets it apart. In other instances, residents see its clearly local control and lack of denominational entanglements ("independent") as its major attraction. Other Distinctive churches are identified by their program focus (the "social action" church, the church with the "healing ministry").

People who want to participate in and/or be identified with the emphasis of the Distinctive church are drawn to it, often from a wide area. As a result, Distinctive churches stand or fall almost entirely on their local appeal. Most are neither aided nor hindered by a denominational connection—if they happen to have one. Because they highlight local characteristics, whatever distinguishes the Distinctive church locally governs the appeal it holds for those in its area. When whatever it represents is appealing, the Distinctive church thrives; when its focus is not sufficiently engaging to enough people in its area, the Distinctive church suffers.

Small but growing Distinctive churches include churches identified with theological and social positions that are popular among those who live in rural areas (for example, churches that characterize themselves as "fundamental," "Pentecostal," or "independent"). In fact, in many small towns and rural areas, newly established Distinctive churches centered on popular values find themselves growing while Denominational and Dominant churches are declining. Many pastors and lay leaders in mainline churches are frustrated by their inability to bridge the reputational gap between the Dominant and Denominational churches they serve and the people who now surround them.

In some cases, the obvious denominational connection of the church and pastor seems to be a liability. The largely urban values that now dominate mainstream denominations are not popular among many residents of rural communities. Pastors who serve mainstream churches are often stressed between the culture in which they serve and the denomination with which they are affiliated. Pastors and prospective pastors need to learn how to help small Dominant and Denominational churches widen their appeal to persons who currently are not attracted to these, or any, churches.

Types of Congregations

Our efforts to categorize congregations according to the effects of recent change on them also produced a typology of congregations. Nearly all the congregations served by pastors in our sample are either Dominant or Denominational churches affiliated with a mainline denomination. As we listened to pastors describe the effects of recent social and demographic changes on their congregations, three categories took shape, which we named "Newcomer," "Indigenous," and "Culturally Mixed." We chose those names to reflect the kinds of persons now active in each group of congregations.[2]

Newcomer Congregations

Newcomer congregations are dominated by persons who are relatively new to the areas the congregations serve. Newcomer congregations are most often located in communities where the population is increasing. Many Newcomer congregations served by pastors in our sample are gaining members.

Some small Newcomer congregations seem to attract new members from among those who move into formerly rural areas precisely because these churches still appear to be rural and small. These churches represent the traditional culture many newcomers want to be part of when they move to the kind of area these churches serve. However, as we listened to pastors and lay leaders from these Newcomer churches describe their congregations, we believe the churches in this first group now reflect a culture that has as much or more in common with mainstream, metropolitan, urban United States culture than it does with rural culture.

In many—possibly most—cases, current leaders in Newcomer congregations are drawn both from among newcomers and from those who are native to the area the church serves. In a majority of Newcomer congregations, however, the newcomers have more influence on the direction the church is now taking. Rarely is the reverse true. Perhaps newcomers have begun to dominate the leadership in these congregations because they tend to have more years of formal education, are more articulate, and usually are younger than natives. Those natives who still participate in Newcomer congregations are more likely than other natives to have adopted some of the attitudes and values of mainstream society. In many respects, they seem more like the newcomers than other natives.

Those who are native to the area and who still reflect traditional culture are less likely to be active in small, mainline Newcomer congregations.
When Newcomer congregations reflect urban culture and are dominated
by non-natives, many locals no longer feel comfortable in them. Such locals
either become active in Distinctive congregations, or dropout of church
entirely.[3]

Our interviews with clergy revealed that most seminary-educated ministers, especially those with urban or suburban roots, find Newcomer congregations the easiest small churches to serve. While the Newcomer congregation appears to be rural, the members (and especially the leaders)
reflect many of the values of the larger culture within which the minister
was educated, and with which he or she still identifies.

Interestingly, a majority of the pastors of small churches that area denominational executives identified as "effective" serve Newcomer congregations. Perhaps pastors socialized in mainline denominations are more likely
to know how to be effective in these "urbanized" Newcomer congregations. Or the selection may reflect the executives' perception of what constitutes an effective small church.

Indigenous Congregations

At the opposite end of the spectrum are congregations we call *Indigenous*
congregations. The majority of members active in Indigenous congregations are not newcomers. They are descended from established families in
the area. Their roots often go back three or more generations. And often
nearly all the members of an extended family are members of the same
Indigenous congregation. It is not uncommon for members of one or two
extended families to dominate the life of a small, Indigenous congregation.

Indigenous congregations tend to be located in areas that are farthest
away from any metropolitan areas. Small, mainline churches in such areas
are almost always Indigenous congregations.

During recent decades most small mainline Indigenous congregations
have steadily become smaller as their members have grown steadily older.
These congregations are least likely to replenish aging members through
natural increase. Largely composed as they are of middle-class members,
their children most often leave the community to seek higher education and
employment. Their location in a depopulated area, coupled with their local,

reputational identity as Dominant or Denominational churches, has brought many of them to a state of crisis. "How long can our church continue when most of the members are now too old to produce more descendants?" is a recurrent question one hears in Indigenous congregations.

Small mainline Indigenous congregations rarely benefit from newcomers, because most immigrants to their communities usually are not middle class, either economically or attitudinally. In fact, such newcomers (sometimes called "refugees from the '60s") are likely to be repelled by the mainline churches' apparent connection to the larger society—which these newcomers want to leave behind. Indigenous congregations often are older, smaller, weakened, and their members are anxious and resentful in the face of change. Many are also disappointed by the apparent inability of their denominations to provide insight or support needed to stem the church's decline.

Many pastors and denominational officials with whom we spoke do seem frustrated in their efforts to understand and help small Indigenous congregations. Such congregations *are* difficult ones for seminary graduates to serve—except the few graduates who are indigenous themselves. The non-native pastor finds few with whom to identify either within the congregation or the community at large. In our research, pastors of these congregations often describe themselves (and their families) as excruciatingly lonely. They don't fit locally, and most denominations do not know how to support them.

Culturally Mixed Congregations

In between Newcomer and Indigenous congregations are a group of congregations we call *Culturally Mixed*. These small churches are akin to the fringe churches one finds wherever a metropolitan area is expanding and culturally overrunning a formerly rural area. We use the name "Culturally Mixed churches" to indicate that they are transitional congregations within which two cultures interact. And while some newcomers are active in Culturally Mixed congregations, the long-standing residents clearly dominate in most small churches included in our survey.

As is the case in those areas where Newcomer congregations are dominant, newcomers here want the best of both worlds (for example, they want the income level of metropolitan society with the space—psychic breathing space—of rural life). However, these newcomers are more likely to have negative feelings about the larger society than their counterparts elsewhere. Attitudinally, many of these newcomers have intentionally left the urban society and its lifeways behind (at least so they believe) to embrace a rural lifeway. They cut wood and accept less income in order to be able to live (at least some of the time) away from the urban "rat race."

But these newcomers differ from their counterparts in areas more commonly served by Indigenous congregations. While both groups agree in their pursuit of a simpler lifeway, those who immigrate to the areas served by churches with Culturally Mixed congregations want simplicity combined with a middle-class level of affluence. As a result of this desire, many of them travel out of the area regularly to earn money, and occasionally to enjoy the cultural benefits of the urban society (such as concerts and plays).

Culturally Mixed congregations are often caught in the transitions and conflicts that dominate the areas they serve. Mainline churches in these areas seem to have difficulty maintaining their appeal to long-standing residents since the churches are often perceived as rooted in a larger alien culture. Also, like their counterparts in other areas, churches whose members are middle class are most likely to shrink in size because children from their membership leave the area to seek higher education and better employment opportunities. Such Culturally Mixed congregations find it increasingly difficult to maintain their membership through natural increase. When these churches lose their appeal to those who are native to the area, or are unable to broaden their appeal to attract persons moving into the community, they dwindle in size.

Most ministers of Culturally Mixed congregations in our survey describe such churches as difficult to pastor. In some instances, ministers feel stressed between the local culture of the natives and the more cosmopolitan culture of the denominations to which they are attached. They may even be ambivalent about which culture they want to belong to. Some describe themselves as torn between the desire to adapt their ministry to the needs and culture of the congregations they serve, and the realization that such a commitment may alienate them from their denominational ethos—and even jeopardize their chances for career development. Moreover, locals may take out some of their frustration with the denomination on the minister (especially if he or she is younger) who appears to represent denominational values and policies with which they are not in sympathy.

Finally, stressed as they are between two cultures, and sometimes eroded of resources and leadership, Culturally Mixed congregations are especially vulnerable to conflict. Ministers in our survey who serve in these congregations are painfully aware of their lack of conflict management skills.

Whether a small church is viewed as Dominant, Denominational, or Distinctive and whether it currently is dominated by Newcomers, Locals, or is Culturally Mixed shapes the kind of ministry that is possible and likely to be effective in that congregation. Students and pastors who understand the dynamics associated with various types of small congregations will be better able to identify where they can serve effectively. We now turn our attention to the particular issues faced by pastors who receive calls to small congregations.

PERSONAL ISSUES RURAL AND SMALL-TOWN PASTORS FACE

Loneliness, isolation, and a sense of spiritual inadequacy are the personal difficulties most often mentioned by pastors of small congregations. Clergy who serve in all kinds of churches describe the ministry as a lonely occupation. But pastors of rural churches seem to be particularly vulnerable to loneliness for several reasons.

Sources of Loneliness

First, *rural and small-town culture tends to be more traditional and can be more confining than urban culture.* Pastors who serve in rural and small-town churches told us they are rarely able to function outside the well-defined role expectations within which they are seen by those with whom they live. The rural pastor is known to be a minister by all. Everyone relates to the rural and small-town pastor as "the minister" everywhere he or she goes.

As a result, such ministers say they are always "on duty." Even local persons beyond their congregations who might become friends are encouraged by the culture to relate to the minister strictly as a minister. If a pastor finds friends within the church membership, and then spends an unusual amount of time with those persons, other church members may accuse the pastor of favoritism. In such circumstances, many pastors feel the only way to escape the demands of ministry is to withdraw, to spend time alone. When such withdrawal is not sought, it can lead to feelings of loneliness.

Second, *rural social patterns tend to exclude newcomers*. Rural communities are notorious for their slow acceptance of new persons. Pastors who seek to break out of their pastoral role to build social relationships with long-term residents quickly discover that they are viewed as outsiders, and subject to the same constraints as all non-natives are.

Social relationships in rural communities tend to occur within families, and to be confined to family members. Except for official church and community functions, holiday parties, picnics, and other social occasions are planned and carried on within extended families. Unless they are fortunate enough to have family close by, pastors and their families are not included in any of these networks. The snub is usually not intentional. People generally do not think about inviting the pastor and family. They would feel awkward with them present at a family gathering, not necessarily because the pastor is a pastor, but because the pastor and family are not "one of us."

A third source of loneliness faced by many rural pastors is *the distance that separates them from their own extended families*. Most of those entering the ministry today have roots in metropolitan areas, and most of the entry-level pastorates are in small congregations. Thus, a significant proportion of those who now serve rural and small-town churches are located some distance away from their own extended families.

Finally, *the typical minister's schedule and limited economic means also contribute to his or her loneliness*. Most holidays involve added work for clergy. Even civic holidays (like Memorial Day and Independence Day) often include occasions when the minister is expected to be present to perform official duties. When others have time off from work and are free to travel to share a holiday with their families, ministers are confined by added responsibility. Even when the holiday is past and ministers have more personal freedom, many clergy are still not able to go away with their families. Spouses and children are usually on the same schedule as the rest of the community. Once the holiday is past, and the minister is available, an employed spouse must return to work and school-age children must go back to school. Again, the pastor is alone.

In talking with rural and small-town pastors in our sample, we have concluded that pastors tend to spend their free time with other pastors not only because they share common understandings and are most comfortable with their peers, but also because pastors are the only other persons who share the same schedule.

Geographical Isolation

The loneliness of many rural and small-town pastors is compounded by geographical isolation. Distance from recreation and cultural events is especially difficult for pastors whose roots are not rural. Many pastors in our sample who have moved from metropolitan areas to rural areas described how much they and their spouses miss being close to museums, concert halls, and other sources of entertainment and stimulation.

Church members who are native to a rural area are often unable to appreciate how much an urban-bred person hungers for such stimulation. (After sharing her wonderful experiences of a recent trip to the city with a rural-bred church member, one spouse was greeted with this response: "I can't understand why you wanted to be away; it was nice here all week.") Many rural people are sufficiently nurtured by their relationships, and simply by being in a space that is familiar, where they have spent their entire lives. They also often produce their own entertainment in the form of activities like games, square dances, singing, and playing instruments. Their proficiency in homemade entertainment replaces the urban person's cultivated appreciation for museums and concerts. Many cannot appreciate why anyone would want or need to go away, or why it might be difficult for the urban-bred minister to join into what feels so natural to them.

Pastors, their spouses, and children who do not have rural roots need to be prepared and equipped to live in a remote area when they accept ministry in a rural or small-town church. Some of those who move into a rural area will find they fit naturally within rural culture—and thrive. Others will find rural and small-town life confining and lonely. When the ministry is difficult and demanding and the pay is low (as it is in most small congregations), such pastors (and, if they are married, their spouses and children), may find rural living oppressive.

Spiritual Inadequacies

Finally, many ministers in our survey are embarrassed and frustrated by what they feel is inadequate spiritual formation. In several other studies we have conducted among mainline clergy, pastors described a lack of spiritual formation as their most significant problem.

Such spiritual uncertainty may be especially painful for mainline, rural clergy, surrounded as they are by rapidly growing congregations that represent fundamentalist values and understandings. Pastors and members of these congregations often seem clear about what they believe, and are quite vocal about their relationship with God. The relative spiritual ambiguity the denominational minister experiences is not easy to bear—especially when confronted by church members who ask, "How come they [the fundamentalists] are doing so well, and we're not?"

The current growing concern of mainline denominations to help clergy with spiritual formation is especially important for pastors of small congregations in rural areas. Most pastors of small, rural churches serve in congregations that are declining and struggling in the face of fundamentalist congregations that are growing. Without a sense of spiritual certainty, it is not easy for a minister in such circumstances to go on day after day.

Necessary Understandings and Attitudes

From the perspective of those who responded to our survey, well-equipped pastors of small congregations

- know how to live and work in rural culture
- understand the nature of the small church
- know how to do administration in a small church
- know how to develop church program (for instance, stewardship, education, outreach) with limited resources
- know how to manage conflicts

However, even when these pastors feel well equipped for ministry in some of these, they also describe other areas where they feel deficient in understanding and/or skill.

Most of the surveyed pastors feel their seminary preparation was adequate in such traditional areas as theology, biblical studies, and preaching, but did not provide them with some essential insights and skills they need to practice ministry in small congregations. The typical pastor serving in a small church feels he or she is a capable theologian and preacher, but feels woefully inadequate when confronted by a conflict between two factions, or a Sunday school of seven children, or a congregation that seems to have little or no concern for global justice.

Pastors told us that what they learned in most seminary or continuing education courses, designed to provide pastors with practical skills, has not

does not need to be perfect. But he or she does need to be able to function as an emotionally mature pastor who will not do damage either to him- or herself or to others in the course of ministry.

In addition to basic psychological health and emotional maturity, our research points up the need for pastors to be psychologically and emotionally suited for the ministry they envision. For example, pastors need to possess not only listening skills, but the patience to hear out sometimes slow-to-speak local people in order to discover both why "we've always done it that way" and then to identify suitable changes. Appropriate changes endure in the life of a small congregation because they are suited to the lifeway of the people who compose it. Possible and suitable changes do not usually become apparent quickly to a pastor. Persistence, it turns out, is usually essential to effective ministry with small congregations, and it is to that issue that we turn next.

Persistent and Untypical Ministers

To become an effective pastor in a small congregation takes time. Nearly all the ministers identified as unusually effective either by other pastors of small churches or by lay leaders we surveyed have one characteristic in common: they currently serve, or in the past have served, the same small congregation(s) for many years—often a decade or more. Effective pastors of small churches are willing and able to persist in a ministry.

Why is longevity so vital? Perhaps because genuine appreciation of the lifeways of those who live in a culture is essential before a pastor is able to identify and facilitate changes or developments that are appropriate and possible for those who compose the churches in that culture. From our interviews it appears that the most effective rural pastors appreciate and understand the lifeways of the people they pastor. They identify with and enter into the lifeways and culture of those with whom they serve. They see themselves as one of them; they stand *with* them, not above them. Such understanding, identity, and trust usually require many years to develop— especially when a pastor is "from away."

Effective pastors of small churches are usually *not* achievement oriented. And in this respect they are different from most clergy today. The most popular current models of ministry, the professional and managerial models, seem to us to be largely inappropriate, out-of-culture models for pastors of small churches, especially pastors of rural, small churches. A professional identity creates respect in an urban culture where professionals abound. In a rural culture where professionals are rare and usually are people "from away," a professional identity creates distance from most people. If a rural pastor insists on a "professional" identity, a majority of his or her neighbors are put off. They see that pastor as someone beyond them, whose person and knowledge are not accessible to them.

A managerial identity is also usually not helpful. "Manager" is an organizational or corporate identity. Most organizations and corporate systems rooted in the larger society place rural people and institutions at the bottom or on the fringe. Rural people typically experience big government, corporations, and institutions as insensitive and inconsiderate of their needs and circumstances. A pastor who functions like a manager engages these negative feelings; such a pastor's concern for organizational effectiveness feels cold, calculating, and alien.

Effective rural, small-church pastors usually forge a model of ministry with elements drawn from biblical-theological sources on the one hand, and from the culture in which they are practicing ministry on the other. They are culturally sensitive, as well as biblically astute. Their models are indigenous, not imposed. They serve long enough in an area to discover cultural ways that need to be included in a locally workable way of ministry.

Several years ago a middle-aged student who gave up farming to attend Bangor Seminary and prepare for ministry with rural congregations shared such a culturally indigenous model of ministry. After some experience as a student pastor in small congregations he decided that a rural pastor in a small church is more like a dairy farmer than a professional or a manager. His own words describe why:

> When I would go to the barn on a winter morning, I never knew what I would find. A cow might be down [sick]; or the power out; or a water line frozen. I had to be ready to deal with anything, to fix whatever needed fixing. I never had enough time to do things right. I was always short of money; I never seemed to catch up with my bills. I was happy when I could just keep things going. But I loved that work and that life. While I never seemed to get ahead, I felt that what I did mattered.
>
> That's what ministry in a small church is like. You keep it going. You don't seem to accomplish much beyond helping others

keep going. If you look carefully, sometimes you can see how much the church matters—how it helps people make it. Ministry is like going to the barn every day. You don't get ahead; but you know it matters.

Holding up such a model of ministry developed from within, rather than imposed upon, rural culture is helpful to rural pastors for two reasons: the way the model encourages them to see themselves as pastors, and what the model implies they will be able to accomplish.

Managerial and professional models of ministry that have their roots in metropolitan culture are alien to rural life. Such models encourage pastors to measure their performance against norms like growth and achievement. The dairy farmer model, by contrast, encourages pastors to evaluate their ministry in terms of the quality of their care-giving and their ability to make do with the resources available to them. The core values in this model are not metropolitan values like organizational growth and development, but rural values like persistence and conservation. This model also encourages pastors to think of ministry as a long-term investment, to recognize that returns in a rural ministry are likely to come only after many years of nurturing.

Those who hold to metropolitan cultural models of ministry that emphasize growth and achievement find abundant biblical evidence to support their perspectives. We believe there is equally convincing biblical evidence that supports the rural culture-based models we see many of the most effective pastors of small churches acting out (for instance, Jesus' focus on a few disciples and his great patience and persistence in his ministry with them). Speed, achievement, advancement, and mobility are not appropriate cultural norms for rural ministers. Those who hold such priorities would do well to stay away from ministry with small churches, especially *rural* small churches.

Obviously, ministry with a small church is a kind of ministry in which only some pastors will thrive. Pastors survive and thrive in a rural ministry when that ministry is suitable for them, and when they plan to stay long enough to become culturally integrated. Of course, pastors (and spouses) who *require* the stimulation of urban culture usually do not do well in a rural ministry. In response to our survey pastors indicated that they move from rural parishes either because they are frustrated by rural life and/or find ministry with a small congregation too confining. They dislike the isolation;

the location seems too remote from cultural activities and adequate medical services; educational opportunities seem poor; they miss the stimulation of colleagues; or they believe their salaries are not adequate.

But a pastor whose personal make-up equips him or her for ministry with a small church, and who *wants* to survive and thrive in rural ministry, and *plans* to do so likely will. One who plans to stay will invest deeply in forming friendships and establishing solid, culturally appropriate patterns of ministry. While the economic rewards given to rural pastors are usually not so great as those given to pastors of larger, urban churches, rural pastors who invest in their churches often find their churches investing in them. Likely the pastor's spouse (if she or he has one) will have to work to help support the household. A pastor (and spouse) who feels called to remain in a rural ministry may discover that she or he needs to emulate a common rural way of life and develop several sources of income. Denominational rules that make it difficult for pastors to accept other employment may be out of step with both rural culture and rural economics. Many rural families have developed innovative lifeways and happily work hard at a variety of jobs to be able to continue to live where they live. So can pastors and their families. Such pastors are likely to do well and to remain in rural ministry, because they fit.

Essential Skills

Finally, our research indicates that there are some essential skills pastors of small congregations need to possess to minister effectively. Unfortunately many pastors and lay leaders become fully conscious of their need for these skills only at the point that they realize they (or their pastors) lack them! Both lay leaders and clergy see the widest gaps between a pastor's need for skills and his or her sense of having these skills in two very important areas: (1) knowing when and how to facilitate change, and (2) knowing how to manage conflict. Both groups also indicate pastors have difficulty accepting and working within the unique dynamics of small churches, and are not adequately equipped to develop effective education and worship within the limited resources available in most small congregations. Nor do they see pastors adequately prepared to help their congregations develop better stewardship and increase income.

Regrettably, few of the many resources designed to be helpful to pastors and churches are designed with the needs of small congregations in mind. Our study of available program resources reveals that most materials rarely address the needs of small congregations, especially rural small congregations. Educational materials usually assume a pool of educationally qualified teachers able to devote considerable time to preparation. Stewardship materials assume that the needs of the church will be presented by visitors who make calls on church families and who have ample print or other visual resources available to them. Denominational mission literature points up mission as a "global" enterprise in which local persons are asked to participate by becoming informed and giving money.

Such materials and the approaches they imply are largely unsuitable for use in most small congregations. Most of those who teach Sunday school in small congregations carry so many responsibilities in church and community life that they have little time to invest in preparation. Members of small congregations characteristically make their stewardship decisions like an extended family, by meeting together in a congregational gathering where they consider the needs of the church and its ministries, and decide together how they will respond. They prefer to enter into mission through direct action. "Global" mission makes sense (feels real) to them only insofar as it becomes linked to a local ministry they have experienced.

Obviously all of us who prepare and support pastors need to do a better job of providing pastors of small churches with the skills and resources they need to minister well. We offer five specific suggestions as to how this can be achieved:

1. Being able to identify which pastors will be able to serve well in small congregations is the key. We need to learn how to help prospective pastors make realistic choices—at the seminary, as well as within denominational units. Those who opt for ministry in small congregations need to do so on the basis of solid self-understanding and awareness of what ministry will be like in a rural culture and a small church. They need to be familiar with various types of small churches and to know in which they can serve best.
2. Placing students with able and healthy pastors and lay leaders for their field experience is indispensable. In such placements, students can learn from their mentors not only how to do ministry in small congregations, but how to take care of themselves as well.
3. At the seminary level, we need to encourage those who plan to minister in small congregations to acquire necessary practical skills.

Prospective pastors of small congregations need to learn how to carry on administration, develop religious education, manage conflict, carry on local missions, and so forth, within the limited resources available in most small congregations.

4.   Those who begin ministry in small congregations, and who have not had the benefit of a seminary program focused on small congregations, need a solid orientation program.

5.   Facilitating support relationships among clergy who serve in small congregations should be a major agenda for denominational units.

Above all of these suggestions, however, developing a positive and adequate understanding of the small church seems especially important. Our conversations with church leaders in the process of sharing the research data we have gathered lead us to believe that many still do not appreciate the qualitative difference between rural and urban culture, and between small and large churches. The commonly accepted designation of rural areas as "nonmetropolitan" encourages negative perspectives. Rural areas are seen as less populated, less developed, less sophisticated. People and institutions in rural areas are seen as lacking and lagging.

Within some denominational circles small congregations, especially rural small congregations, also do not have a positive identity. Pastorates with rural small churches are viewed as being "on the bottom." Pastors who are appointed to rural parishes or who accept calls to these churches believe they are seen by denominational officials, and often by their colleagues, as less able.

Such perspectives deny the potential of small churches and their pastors. The research we have completed among lay leaders and some of the most able pastors of small rural churches indicates that these pastors and lay leaders hold positive attitudes toward small churches and rural areas. Most members of rural small congregations have chosen to join and remain with these congregations because the churches reflect values, opportunities for ministry, and a way of life that they affirm. They see small churches as churches filled with potential. And many are faithfully living out that potential in their ministries. As we have come to know these pastors and lay leaders in small churches, we have come to respect them as well. From them we have learned that small churches can be great churches. They are truly God's disciples carrying on faithful ministry.

Notes

1. Supported by a grant from Lilly Endowment Inc., we mailed an 11-page questionnaire to 116 pastors of small congregations in northern New England and northeastern New York. These pastors had been previously identified as effective by their colleagues and/or regional executives and we surveyed them because we believed they would be reliable sources of insight. Given the complexity and time needed to complete the questionnaire, we were surprised and gratified by the large proportion of pastors who responded. Over 80 completed questionnaires were received from the 116 pastors surveyed: a 70 percent response rate! After extensive analysis of 77 questionnaires, we interviewed approximately one-third of those who responded in order to clarify our perceptions. This essay is based on analysis of both the questionnaires and the interviews. Although our survey only covered those in a limited geographical area, we feel that many of these findings are likely to be applicable to other areas of the country as well, and this essay has been edited to reflect such an understanding.

2. We also noted that congregations in each category appear more frequently in a certain geographical area. Because of the large number of Maine congregations in our sample and our greater familiarity with Maine geography, we were able to describe these areas more precisely in Maine. If our sample had included more congregations from other areas, we believe we could associate types with specific geographical areas in other states as well. We hope our description of those types is clear enough to enable those from other states who read this report to determine where each type appears most frequently in their area.

3. In fact, on the basis of our research, we believe that some of the growth of independent, fundamentalist Distinctive churches in Maine can be attributed to the waning appeal of mainline churches to native Mainers.

4. In this final section, we want to share the suggestions we received in written form and in interviews with nearly 50 lay leaders in small congregations scattered throughout northern New England and northeastern New York, and correlate those findings with the responses we received from the pastors that we surveyed.

5. Once they had indicated how important they believe the attributes are, we asked lay leaders and pastors to go through the various items again and indicate the relative sense of adequacy they feel as pastors, or, as lay leaders, perceive in pastors of small churches. Again we averaged the scores. Then we *compared* the average score for sense of adequacy with the average score from level of importance for each attribute by *subtracting them*. In the table below the attributes are ranked according to the average difference between sense of adequacy and estimate of importance of each attribute. In the first list, for example, compared with their sense of its importance, lay leaders see clergy as most adequate in their ability to be "outspoken and direct," and least adequate in their ability to be "good listeners." Clergy have similar estimates.

Survey Results

Personal Characteristics

Lay	Clergy	
1	1	Outspoken and direct
2	2	Wants to and able to live in area where church is located
3	12	Patient; able to live with little or no change
4	5	Able to live in a relatively isolated area
5	13	Self-starter
6	8	Sensitive and compassionate
7	14	Tough; NOT thin-skinned
8	4	Creative
9	9	Willing and able to live on lesser than average income
10	7	Good sense of humor; doesn't take self too seriously
11	6	Able to share power and authority
12	3	Psychologically strong and emotionally secure
13	10	Genuinely caring
14	11	Engenders trust and confidence
15	15	Good listener

Characteristics of Spouse

Lay	Clergy	
1	1	Spouse wants to and able to live in area where church is located.
2	2	Spouse willing and able to live on lower than average income

Piety

Lay	Clergy	
1	1	Openly accepts authority of scripture
2	4	Deep and obvious commitment to Jesus Christ
3	3	Evidences strong faith
4	2	Shares his/her faith easily and openly

Approach to Ministry (Attitude)

Lay	Clergy	
1	1	Concerned and involved beyond the local level, in the church at large
2	3	Willing and able to remain as pastor of parish for many years

3	2	Able to work cooperatively with other pastors, as part of a team
4	4	Willing to meet practical as well as spiritual needs of people
5	10	More concerned about persons than program
6	6	Willing to be responsive to and work within local culture
7	7	More concerned about quality in church life than numbers
8	9	Likes to visit church members
9	8	Willing and able to develop program with limited resources and leadership
10	5	Flexible, not rigid, approach to ministry

Skills for Ministry

Lay	Clergy	
1	5	Knows how to work with community organizations and agencies
2	4	Knows how to work effectively with an inadequate and/or inefficient church building
3	2	Skilled planner and organizer
4	1	Effective preacher
5	9	Knows how to provide for his/her own self-care and nurture
6	3	Skilled counselor
7	8	Knows how to develop effective education and worship within the limited resources available in a small congregation
8	6	Skilled in developing stewardship; knows how to help church increase income and find options within limited income
9	7	Accepts and is able to work within the unique dynamics of small congregation
10	10	Knows how and when to facilitate change
11	11	Knows how to manage conflict

Previously published in seven parts in The Five Stones *(Winter 1994—Summer 1995); used by permission. The original version of this material appeared in* The Open Door, *a publication of Bangor Theological Seminary.*

Chapter 2

UNDERSTANDING AUTHORITY
IN
SMALL CHURCHES

Richard Griffin

Adjusting to the small or rural church after attending seminary is perhaps the major hurdle for new pastors. The rural community is concerned, obviously, about agriculture; the typical seminarian has never needed to have such concern. The bred-in-the-bone background of rural life affects people in ways the average seminarian can only imagine—the lack of money and the corresponding need to make do, the frustrations of being unable to price your own goods, the stress of never being able to take a vacation. For someone born and raised in suburbia, where the vast majority of people work for someone else and the entrepreneur is the exception rather than the rule, this rural worldview appears almost unnatural. Add to this the different, much lower general education level than exists in the seminary community, and adjustment to the small church becomes an enormous task.

These differences, however, can be anticipated. Preparing for them takes work, research, prayer, and imagination, but it can be done. In fact, any reasonably diligent seminarian can even prepare for the different *expectations* of the rural church. Most such churches, for example, expect that the pastor will function as a sort of religious hireling—a chaplain carrying out the religious duties of the congregation—rather than as a pastor or a leader. And while seminary courses focus on the role of the pastor in the *leading* of churches, a sympathetic between-the-lines reading of the essays in this book (or other books on the small church) would alert the student that the situation is not the same as course work usually indicates. Thus, to a certain extent, the seminarian can prepare for the obvious and expectable differences between the small church and the seminary community.

What the seminarian will *not* expect, however, is that the rural church has an entirely different perception of reality than does the seminary community. Further, if she or he enters the rural pastorate unaware of this difference, unaware of what this perception *is*, the seminarian will make bad mistakes, damaging mistakes, simply because she or he is *not operating in the same world as the parishioners*. Nor, by and large, does seminary give the student any framework and paradigm within which to interpret these different realities. And this lack continues despite the fact that most of the mistakes a pastor makes in the rural church can be avoided by a better understanding of the rural worldview.

This essay attempts to address that lack by focusing on one of the more important differences between the rural church and the seminary community: *the nature of authority*. We will explore the nature of the small town and how that is reflected in the allocation of authority and allegiance, and how the small-town church, in turn, reflects that reflection. We will draw some enlightening contrasts between the small town and the seminary and discuss some of the practical implications of these contrasts. Most important, we will describe a paradigm for small church decision making, so the new pastor can know what to expect.

THE NATURE OF AUTHORITY IN SMALL TOWNS

Most small towns are *monolatrous*; that is, the people in them have one uniform idol, one that manifests itself in a variety of ways. For example, the new pastor often complains that the lines separating groups of people are clear and hard and fast—that very few people cross these lines. That pastor perceives accurately—but the firmness of those socioeconomic lines is only possible because everyone in the town holds to the same values and lives according to the same concerns. In short, everyone worships the same idol. This idol can vary from town to town, but in most cases it can be labeled "respectability"—acceptance in and by the community. Furthermore, the drive toward respectability and the fear of doing anything that might cost you your standing in the community becomes greater as the size of the town grows smaller.

Respectability, at least as I have observed it, has three components: (1) Ownership; (2) Community Support; and (3) Local History. A satisfactory level of attainment in each of these components is necessary to be respectable—and each component admits of subdivisions into categories and subcategories.

OWNERSHIP

For example, one community classifies Ownership into four different categories. In each category, subcategories exist, with the farmer at the top of the respectability heap in each subcategory (see *Table A*).

Table A: Categories of Ownership

Employing Owner: owns sufficient resources not only to provide for himself and his family, but also to employ other individuals year-round

Farmer: owns enough land, machinery, livestock to need hired hands

Banker: employs others to do telling, accounts, and so forth

Merchant: contractors, store owners who employ others year round for various purposes

Self-Employed Owner: owns sufficient resources to support self and family without working for someone else

Farmer: supports self and family with own land, machinery, and livestock; may occasionally hire extra help for special jobs

Single-person businesses: tractor mechanic, garage owner; owns business and home, but no farmland; self-employed

Employed Owner: owns resources, but not enough to support himself or his family; works for someone else

Farmer: owns land/livestock/machinery or any combination thereof, but not enough of it to support his family; works outside the farm at the post office or a feed lot or the like

Teacher, Factory worker, etc.: owns home and perhaps some land, but works full time at a job and does no farming himself

——————————————————— (Respectability cut-off line)

Employed Non-Owner: owns no resources, but works
School Superintendent: works, but lives in housing provided by the schoo
system
School Principal, Pastors: work, but live in provided housing
Permanent hired hands: work, but live in employer-owned housing (the nor-
　　　　mal situation in our area)

Unemployed Non-Owner

Ownership is perhaps the most important component of respectability. An individual who wishes to have any influence in the community at all simply must be an owner. Otherwise, he (or, occasionally, she) is viewed as a transient, not to be trusted with the important affairs of the town. Note too that in the rural community it is the husband's standing that, with rare exceptions, determines the family's respectability in the community.

COMMUNITY SUPPORT

Community is that component of respectability dealing with the amount of time and energy an individual spends doing those activities the community values as an expression of its corporate importance. This component, too, admits of categorizing (see *Table B*).

Table B: Categories of Community Support

Active Support—participating in the events the town values
　　　Holding political office—school board, town council
　　　Booster Club activities
　　　Coaching Little League
　　　Showcase landscaping

Normal Support—regular attendance at events the community values
　　　Church services
　　　Athletic events
　　　Community choir
　　　Flower gardening

Minimal Support—attending only rare events
   Weddings
   Funerals
   Graduation
   Keeping lawn mowed, walks shoveled

———————————————————————— (Respectability cut-off line)

Refusal of Support—the individual is perceived as not valuing the values
the community holds
   Refusal to attend ball games, funerals, graduation
   Lawns gone to seed
   Broken machinery left in yard

Note that within categories, the subcategories are all of relatively equal weight. Thus, an individual who coaches Little League will fall into the same category, and will be as respectable in this component, as the chief councilman. Another point to notice is the role of the appearance of an individual's property in determining respectability. This is perhaps best explained by viewing all of these activities as a measure of an individual's pride in the community.

LOCAL HISTORY

Local history, on the other hand, admits of only two categories (see *Table C*), although the subcategories are more numerous.

Table C: Categories of Family History

Reared in the Community
   Family has history of respectability, back several generations
   Family new to the area since your birth, but you grew up in the school
      system
   Married to someone reared in the community
   Reared in community, left, but returned

Reared outside community, but manager of Farmer's Co-op (an interesting anomaly!)

——————————————————————— (Respectability cut-off line)

Reared outside the Community
School Superintendent
Principal
Pastor
Hired Hands
Other

While this is the only component that admits of upward mobility (a given individual cannot change categories upward unless she or he marries within the community), it is also the least important component of respectability. The pastor who becomes an owner, who actively supports the community, will find that while others do not forget that she or he is not native to the community, they will tend to overlook that fact.

General Notes: These categories can also be ranked in order of importance: Ownership most important, followed by Community Support, and then by Family History. Note that each of these categories admits of a cut-off line: individuals who fall below any of these lines in any category will not be considered respectable. Their opinions will be given very little weight, and they will have very little influence on decision making.

***

Why such detail? Are these components and categories really so important? Yes, for everyone of any standing in the community, everyone who holds any power in the community, holds to these standards intuitively. These standards are not promulgated, nor are they necessarily articulated. Some individuals might even deny they exist. However, they inform every breath taken and every decision made: social decisions, political decisions, and ministry decisions. Because of this the rural pastor should have *both* this structure and the pastors standing in it clearly in mind before attempting any change in the church.[1]

All of these facts have a direct bearing on how the pastor operates in the rural church.

AUTHORITY STRUCTURES OF SMALL CHURCHES

Small churches reflect small towns in their concerns. The monolithic worship of respectability has a direct impact on the kinds of decisions a small church is willing to consider. Because church attendance is one of the accepted means of showing support for the community, no one wants the church to disturb the status quo in that community—least of all the people who attend church.

Now this is not to say that people attend church with the stated purpose of being accepted in the community. That was true even as recently as one generation ago, but no longer. It is to say that the church will not under normal circumstances (that is, anything short of a Holy Spirit-sent revival) do *anything* that would be unacceptable to the majority of the members of the community. In practice this means that evangelism will be a very low priority. Any outreach will be tailored so as to be as inoffensive as possible, even to the point of rendering that outreach ineffective. It also means that any attempt to break down the social lines that divide the acceptable from the unacceptable—hired men from landowners, for example—will be met with extreme suspicion and even hostility. Except in very rare cases, ministries or programs that would change the existing social structure in any way will simply not be accepted.

Because everyone in the small church operates within the same worldview, decisions and authority in the church are based on politics and political realities, not upon ideas. This is perhaps the hardest transition for a seminarian to make. Seminary culture is *ideological*—it gives allegiance to the notion that ideas are (or at least should be) the determiners of behavior.

In the small church, however, authority stems from *politics*. People give their allegiance to *institutions* and to other *people*, not to ideas or to doctrine. Thus, for example, you find the women's missionary society going on as it always has—and those involved believe even at the subconscious level that this is as it *should* be. Tradition, family influence and heritage, individual tenure and service to the church: these are the determiners of allegiance and loyalty and, through them, behavior. Against such a battery of concerns, a mere idea has no chance for influence.

While the seminarian or new pastor might lament this situation, certain facts about small town life make it unavoidable, perhaps even unchangeable. People in small towns have long memories. They are no better at forgiving than people elsewhere and it is impossible for them to *forget* a hurt because they see the offending individual every week. When you've had a fight with someone, there simply aren't enough other people to hide behind. This same lack of people means there are very few social circles: a given individual has very few options for friends and acquaintances. To top it all off, what circles exist are closed—if an individual gets kicked out of one, she or he has no assurance of finding another.

As a result, very few people are willing to provoke conflict. Translated, this means that very few people are willing to fight for change, on the basis of a new idea or on the basis of the truth alone. For if an individual pushes too hard for a new thing, she or he could very well find him- or herself without friends at all.

This is especially true in churches that have a history of calling seminarians as pastors (most rural churches have such a history). Ideas and pastors, after all, come and go, but the people in the community stay. If an individual falls in behind the pastor, fights for change, and as a result is expelled from his or her social circle, what will he or she do when the pastor leaves? For no matter how respectable an individual is, if he or she is perceived as a boat-rocker, all influence and acceptability are forfeit. Thus, even those people in the small church who are ideological, willing to change their behavior on the basis of a new truth or idea, soon become powerless to effect change in the church or in other people. They become shunned and almost outcast because they are no longer perceived as respectable.

PRACTICAL CONSEQUENCES

First, despite the possible distastefulness of the idea, a pastor working for change in the small church will have to work *politically*. Many of the writings on the small church describe the political process of change in the small church. The pastor must *not* attempt to work any other way. (That is, at least not organizationally. None of this is meant in any way to exclude the possibility of change brought about by true revival!) The finest preaching in the world will not change the small church: all the pastor's preaching (presentation of truth) does is give him or her the right to enter the political process of the church.

Second, the change process in the small church is subject to the strengths and weaknesses of the political process. One of the strengths of this process is that if the *pastor* can effect change by working through the leaders of the church, that change is much more likely to be permanent. One of the weaknesses is that the pastor will probably be able to effect, at most, only *one* major change during his or her tenure. (There are some rare exceptions to this rule, but it is unwise to *plan* on being one of them.)

Third, the pastor should work on the most basic change needed. This is not always the most obvious or glaring deficiency in the church.[2] But given that the pastor in a small town can probably effect only one major change, she or he should look for the root problem in the church and concentrate on that.

Fourth, once the pastor has targeted the area in which change is needed, she or he should work toward that change *alone*. The pastor may lay the groundwork for the next minister by mentioning all of the things she or he is concerned about. The pastor may speak about evangelism, mutual love, forgiving others, refraining from passing judgment—anything in which she or he sees a need. The pastor may even preach on these things so that the next minister isn't starting from scratch. But the pastor of the rural church needs to focus all his or her efforts toward change on effecting the most basic *change* his or her church needs to make.

Finally, the rural pastor needs to remember in all ministry that the political structure in the community and the church is in place because it *works*. It achieves what is the bottom line for most of your people: the church stays open. The place in which your congregation grew up, of which they have fond family memories, fond personal memories—this place keeps its doors open. Change, even toward more biblical behavior patterns, is seen as threatening that success. Most churches will let the pastor get away with one change, but you need to be aware that you are threatening what is for some of them the single most important institution in their lives.

NOTES

1. I doubt that this point can be overemphasized simply because it is very hard for a seminary student to grasp the monolithic quality of small-town culture. The seminary is usually located in a polydolatrous setting (Chicago's North Shore, for example). A preacher (or student) can look around and find demonstrations of idolatry everywhere and, moreover, demonstrations of *different* idolatries. To the man who worships power the pastor can say, "Look around you. Do you see those who are worshiping money?" and the power worshiper can then say, "Yes, I see that is idolatry." The pastor can point to the prestige worshiper and have the money

worshiper say, "Yes, I can see that's idolatry." In this way, the pastor can sneak in the back door, so to speak, and suggest to the individual involved that he, too, is an idolater.

This approach is impossible in the rural town. The pastor can point and point and point, but people will not see anything they recognize as idolatry in others. Simply because everyone pursues respectability, no one can recognize that this pursuit limits their ability to pursue God.

2. For example, evangelism is almost always a problem in the rural church for reasons mentioned above. The church may give a huge proportion of its budget to foreign missions (up to 40 percent!) but very little to local, in-town evangelism (often less than 1 percent). Nor will it make up that lack of giving by effort and energy. A glaring problem? Yes. The most basic problem? Not in my current church. Here our most basic problem is lack of prayer. A deeper prayer life in my people would make it much easier for all the other pieces to fall into place: so *that's* the change I am working toward.

Originally published in Action Information *17, no. 1 (January/February 1991): pp. 19-22.*

Chapter 3
FIVE DISCOVERIES
ABOUT
SMALL-TOWN MINISTRY

Lawrence W. Farris

A few years ago, as I commemorated my ninth anniversary of ministry in a small town, I found thoughts gathering on what I had learned about ministry in a community of about 7,500 souls, particularly with the 465 members of my church with whom I had sojourned during those years. Although every small town is no doubt unique (a euphemism for "quirky" and "idiosyncratic" as well as for "distinctive in gifts and callings"), I believe my notes have some wider applicability.

1. OUTSIDER STATUS CAN BE VALUABLE

When I first came to Three Rivers, a friend from seminary told me, "Remember, no matter how long you stay, you will always be an outsider." Those words turned out to be the wisest advice I received. Because secrets are hard to keep and memories are long in small towns, the community needs an outsider who takes confidentiality seriously. It is not at all a matter of xenophobia or shunning, but rather that small-town folks need someone outside the family or the neighborhood to whom they can entrust their deepest yearnings, follies, and secrets. Ironically, the way an outsider minister secures a place in a small town is by embracing this role rather than by trying to work his or her way into service clubs, school committees, and the like. Indeed, one of the sadder and least effective ministers I know spent years in a nearby town trying to get into its inner social and political circles, and, once being more or less inside, found himself with little to offer that was not already available in abundance.

Because family relationships are very important in small towns, it is important for the outsider minister to take time to understand the kinship patterns. Woe to the minister who makes an offhand and less-than-flattering remark about someone outside the congregation, only to find out that the individual in question is a cousin or in-law of a parishioner! Congregational boundaries are made porous by the fact that members of extended, multiple-generation families often are considered "members" of the church. The small-town minister often is asked to officiate at funerals, weddings, and baptisms of folks considered part of the church family whom he or she has not met.

Because of this need for an outsider, I found it more difficult to form friendships within the small-town congregation than when I served churches in more suburban or urban settings. To avoid feelings of isolation, friendships with folks beyond the congregation are essential. But more importantly, in this small town I enjoyed the best ecumenical relationships I had ever known with—of course—the other outsider ministers. A lectionary study group here provided profound support and friendships.

Finally, the outsider minister can make small-town folks aware of resources. Again and again I was surprised when people here didn't know about a good restaurant in a nearby city. But that was also true of resources such as therapists or support groups for people with specific needs. As an outsider, I could connect people with resources new to them. In this regard, an appropriate title for the small-town minister would be "parson," a term used in the late medieval period. Often, the parson of a village was the only one who could read and write, and thus connected the village to the larger world by reading and writing needed correspondence. The contemporary parson often shares a similar, if expanded, function in small towns.

2. History Is Important

Small-town people highly value the shared history of their community and congregation. Three days after I arrived, a "matriarch" of the congregation stopped by my home to drop off a copy of an extensive history of the town. In her own inimitable way, she made it clear that I would do well to read and remember the contents of this volume. She also gave me two congregational histories, one written at its centennial and one at its sesquicentennial. She did me a great favor. What she was telling me was that my ministry and leadership would be better received if I understood and respected the stories of those who had been here long before me and who would remain after I had left. Not only was this written history valued in particular by older members of the faith community, it also allowed me to introduce newcomers to that history and thus facilitate their assimilation into the congregation.

Taking my matriarchal saint's cue, I invited some of the elders of the church to sit in the sanctuary and tell me stories about their memories of that space hallowed by their prayers over many years. How else would I have learned that in the 1920s the church had been used as a movie house, with a projection booth hung on the rear wall and a screen suspended up front, because it was the largest room in town? The woman who shared this fact mused that this just might have been the beginning of the congregation's long-standing openness to others using the church's facilities.

I asked some other folks to take me on a driving tour of the community. In a few short hours, I learned that the African-American community in town came from Chicago to live permanently in what were once summer homes, that the town once had a minor-league baseball team and stadium which was a focal point for recreation, and that the first hospital was in the majestic home of a doctor and was known as "Bonnie Castle." I began to grasp the politics and the economy, and how they had evolved. I could understand subtle references in conversation. And I sensed some of the town's cherished values—an acceptance of diversity, a willingness to give back generously to improve the community, and a high esteem for the arts. All of these discoveries helped me fit my ministry more closely to what matters in the town.

I also learned through this valuing of history that small towns prize longevity in pastorates as highly as individual ministerial skills and credentials. I always felt respected here, but it was not until I had been around for six years that I began to be invited to participate in groups which shape the community's life—boards of institutions, important school committees, and so forth.

Furthermore, this valuing of people's pasts, of who they have been, means it is also important to value who they are now. Even if one feels sports are excessively emphasized in our time, a minister needs to go to some football and basketball and soccer games, not only to see the church youth in another context, but also to affirm that the larger life of the town matters. If seen as a gateway into the heart of the community, attendance at Memorial Day ceremonies and homecoming parades is not just one more ministerial chore, but an opportunity to discern what moves and shapes the town's life. Such knowledge will bear much fruit in ministry; ignorance of it can be fatal.

3. Homecoming Is a Powerful Metaphor

An exchange student from Germany living with our family was puzzled by all the hoopla surrounding football homecoming. She simply could not understand what the big deal was. And I shared that puzzlement when I first came here. But homecoming is a multi-dimensional and crucial metaphor. It is a partial antidote to the nagging suspicion that small towns and the people who live in them no longer matter in an urbanizing, suburbanizing, globalizing culture. When recent high school graduates come back for an autumn evening of parades, parties, and football, it supports a sense that "we do matter" to these young people now out in the larger world. When people long gone from the town come back to retire here, as happens with some regularity, those who haven't left are reassured that there are aspects of life here worth returning to. It reminds them about what is good in their town even as the larger world sees such places as either hopelessly quaint or outdated. When the dead are brought back to be buried, folks here tell stories about the deceased and his or her family, and with those memories comes a sense of renewal. In a world rushing toward and anxious about the future, the metaphor of homecoming helps sustain small towns.

4. The Minister Can Build Bridges

There is a fair amount of turf protection in small towns by churches, service clubs, hospitals, schools, and the like, and this has some important implications for ministry. After enough time had passed that I could become significantly involved in groups beyond my congregation, I began to notice that, for example, people active in the hospital often knew little about what was going on in the schools, and vice versa. At first, I chalked this up to everyone having more than enough to do. As time went on, I realized that because resources in a small town are limited—everyone is competing for the same volunteers, charitable donations, and media exposure—a good deal of turf protection is the rule.

In this context outsider ministers can, in addition to the role of parson, act out of a model of ministry embodied by the title *pontifex*—literally, *bridge builder*. I often could bring helpful information from one group to another, put people working on the same issues in touch with each other, and put a few dents in the dividing walls of hostility simply because I had my feet in a number of camps. As an outsider, I was seen as not having a particular ax to grind or side to take. But I also note that to be effective in this crucial role, it is important not to be over-identified with any one group. Once one is labeled as part of "that service club" or as an advocate of "that business," the work of *pontifex* is ruinously compromised.

5. Activities Must Foster "Belonging"

Members of small-town churches tend to value a sense of community more highly than do those in suburban settings, and will support new activities that enhance their sense of belonging. People may well move to suburbs because they value privacy more highly than community in a too busy and crowded world. One reason people stay in small towns is that they like the sense of knowing and being known, of belonging to a community. Thus, new activities that build up a sense of community pride or deepen relationships among people will be embraced. Our congregation had a great time undertaking a several-months-long Heifer Project International Ark Project. The goal was to raise $5,000 to fight hunger, and programs to meet this goal involved the church school, choirs of all ages, and home activities for singles, couples, and families. Although the congregation has a strong, sometimes almost overriding commitment to local mission work, this project to send money far away succeeded because it involved everyone and built an appropriate pride in the faith community. They can look back and say, "Hey, we did that," and it has become part of the congregation's cherished history.

I have been surprised also at how groups can form here around ideas that might not seem particularly welcome in a small and rather conservative town. A church staff member began a group called "Women's Circle of Light," which offered women the opportunity to explore and experience a wide range of worship using diverse, feminine images of God. I was surprised that not a word was said against this group. Then I realized that it met the criterion of helping people deepen their sense of belonging to one another.

These are the five crucial discoveries that greatly enhanced my ministry in this small community. I trust that new ones will continue to make themselves known.

Originally published in Congregations: The Alban Journal *24, no. 6 (November/December 1998): pp. 18-20.*

Chapter 4
TEN WAYS TO BUILD
A HEALTHIER CONGREGATION

Clay Smith

For many years, Hinton Rural Life Center staff have worked with congregational leaders to help build stronger, healthier, more vital churches. Consulting with congregations usually begins with a visioning/planning process and continues with training around the basics of local church development. This article is an attempt to distill our key learnings into 10 components of healthy congregational development for small-membership congregations.

1. *The primary task of church leaders is to assist members in the task of spiritual discernment regarding the congregation's call to ministry.* At Hinton, we begin with several assumptions about congregations. Every congregation, no matter what its size or location, is called to significant ministry. God has placed the gifts, graces, and resources there for ministry. The task of the members is to discern God's call to ministry and to respond to that call. The first task is discerning where the Spirit is leading us. Persons discern the Spirit's leading as they worship together, hear the word preached, pray together, study together, and as they nurture their own devotional lives.

2. *The second task of leaders is to help members get focused around the vision/hope/promise for the future.* This usually takes place in a planning/visioning process where persons can share insights, gather information, and reflect together about the congregation. Next, folks must set priorities and clarify direction for the congregation's energies. No congregation can do everything that is important right now. Where will we focus our attention for the next year or six months?

3. *Self-determination is the key to building strong self-esteem for the congregation.* At Hinton, we believe that the people in the local church are the real experts who know about the church's ministry. It is necessary to build a broad-based decision-making process that includes as many ideas as possible from as many persons as possible in formulating the new vision for ministry.

4. *Persistence will prevail.* Things take time. Significant changes in the life of a congregation usually take three to five years to put into place. The leaders must be realistic about how much time and energy are required to establish new directions for ministry.

5. *Out of the spiritual discernment/reflection/planning/visioning process will come a clear sense of "the right thing" for this church to do at this particular time.* Of all the many good things we could do, what is the one thing that we must do if we want to grow and develop into a healthier, more vital congregation? What is our growing point right now? Every congregation is unique, and the "right thing" will be specific to each congregation.

6. *Congregations must focus on their strengths, what they do well, rather than on their weaknesses.* Take what you already know how to do and build upon it. If you want to expand ministries, use the skills and strengths that you already possess, and figure out how to use them in another way.

7. While there are many new programs and resources available for congregations, *the first priority must always be to take care of the basic building blocks of congregational development.* These basics include such things as an annual planning/visioning process, an annual financial campaign coupled with year-round stewardship education, regular attention to Christian education and the Sunday School, adequate pastoral care and visitation, and quality worship and preaching from week to week.

8. Our staff has discovered that *congregations do better when they do not become dependent upon outside resources.* It is best to build program and ministry that can be self-sustaining. Long-term

dependency relationships undermine self-esteem and do not empower congregations.

9. *Congregations can greatly strengthen their witness when they link up with neighboring congregations in cooperative ventures.* Working together with others helps churches develop more comprehensive and stronger ministries in order to tackle community-wide issues. When congregations come together to share their strengths, everyone wins. Cooperative ministry is especially helpful in enabling congregations to move beyond the nurture ministry focus of a family-style congregation and to reach out to the community.

10. *Pastors, congregations, and denominational leaders must all work together for longer pastoral tenure.* A church that changes pastors every two, three, or four years spends far too much energy on pastoral transitions, saying good-bye to one pastor and getting acquainted with the next one. A pastoral tenure of six to eight years, or longer, will provide stability within which the congregation can focus its energies on building ministry.

Previously published in The Five Stones *(Fall 1997), pp. 7-8, and reprinted by permission of* United Methodist Rural Fellowship Bulletin, *First UMC, 7102 Michigan Ave., Pigeon, Mich. 48755.*

Chapter 5

Fifteen Steps for Leading a Stable Rural Church Off the Plateau

Gary E. Farley

Many ministers are ill-prepared to lead a small rural or village church. The new pastor comes to the pastorate with one set of expectations and understandings and finds a church with a different set. The stage is set for conflict and hurt.[1] You do not want this. The church does not need it. The following are some steps I suggest you take to discover the inner life of the smaller-membership church you serve:

1. The members of the church want to know about you. They want to know about your upbringing, your pilgrimage of faith, your beliefs. Try to be transparent and autobiographical in your messages and conversations. Of course, be sensitive to their taboos and expectations as you do this.

2. Demonstrate real interest in the congregation's "story." One way to do this is by preaching in the morning service a message on the basic tasks of the local church. This approach provides parameters for a talk-back session in the evening for the members to share with you the founding dream and the work of the church. Seek to include discussion of the history of the community. By focusing on change, which they have observed in the life both of the church and of its community, you will stimulate insightful discussion. Weeks later, people likely will be sharing with you anecdotes about events and changes.[2]

3. Identify the "bell cow" (leader). Most rural congregations have experienced times of poor and/or no pastoral leadership. In this vacuum, strong lay leadership has emerged. Encourage this layperson to become your mentor and learn from him/her how the church functions,

how decisions are made, where the "land mines" are. Realize that his or her endorsement of a project you want to see done may be crucial. Although the time may come when disagreement and even estrangement may occur regarding changes you want to initiate, do not seek conflict when cooperation is possible.[3]

4. Use the letters to the seven churches in the book of Revelation to identify strengths and weaknesses common to churches. Devote a message to each church, followed by a forum in which the congregation can discuss the presence of these same strengths and weaknesses in their church. Discuss how they might draw on their strengths to be a more effective church. Discuss how they might address their weaknesses.[4]

5. Involve the church in active, aggressive prayer. Pray that God will help the church use its strengths and overcome its weaknesses in effective ministry.

6. Identify an event or project the church might do successfully. Organize it, do the project, and enjoy it. (Many small churches suffer from a kind of inferiority complex. A successful project may be what is needed to build a sense of confidence).[5]

7. Integrate what you are learning about your church and your community. Give special attention to identifying ministry needs, persons who are unchurched, and those who are without faith.

8. Share your observations and include those observations and vision for the congregation in the list of prayer concerns.

9. Identify the annual events. Rural churches cherish annual events—revival, homecoming, Vacation Bible School, cemetery decoration, Christmas program, community Holy Week observance. Use these events as the core of annual calendar planning. Help the leaders of each event to plan well.

10. Identify other events or projects the church might do, cooperate in, or sponsor. Ask the church to consider and adopt these, then include the

events and/or projects into the planning process. (You will note that here I am addressing what seems to be the basic flaw in many rural churches—the lack of intentionality. Further, in asking the church to adopt an event or project, you will be asking for additional time and money from the people as well as reallocation of existing resources. Risk is involved in this. Hear objections and take them seriously. Seek consensus if at all possible.) When introducing changes like this, take small steps. Encourage the people to do what is best for the church. If opposition arises, ask for a "trial" period for the new project, event, or program. Remember, the people may know better. You can be wrong.

11. Provide skill training for your members as they carry out the changes approved by the congregation. Training then will provide the motivation for and a determiner of the religious education curriculum.

12. Anticipate that the renewed activity and ministry of the church will attract estranged members and some unbelieving persons. Certainly, if the members feel good about their church and its success, they will be talking about it and inviting others to become a part of it. But a problem in many small country churches is that the members are not intentional about including new people—they may be slow to forgive old wrongs. Being forewarned, take steps to prepare, so that you

   • identify the gifts the new persons bring
   • involve them in ministry
   • arrange for their needs to be met
   • forge linkages with the old members
   • provide educational activities and events that will bind the old with the new

13. Be missionary minded. Many small churches slip into a survival men- tality, which seems to hasten their demise. Looking beyond themselves and helping other churches and people restores vision and helps small churches get moving again.[6]

14. Lead the congregation to consider and seek consensus cooperatively on what the will of God is for the church. What ministries will it major on? Who will it seek to evangelize? How will it assist believers in spiri- tual growth?

15. Assist the church in organizing itself and in allocating its resources to do the ministry God has for it to do.

I believe that if you will conscientiously do what these 15 steps call for, you will see God do some wonderful things—in your church, among the unchurched, in the lives of the saints—and in you as well!

NOTES

1. Anthony Pappas, *Entering the World of the Small Church,* revised and expanded edition (Bethesda, Md.: Alban Institute, 2000).

2. See Carl Dudley, *Making the Small Church Effective,* chap. 5 (New York: Abingdon Press, 1979). See also James Hopewell, *Congregation: Stories and Structure* (Philadelphia: Fortress, 1987), and Rockwell Smith, *Rural Ministry and the Changing Community* (New York: Abingdon Press, 1971).

3. Gary Farley, "Where Are You Headed?" *The Baptist Program* (September 1988), 8.

4. Gary Farley, "And Now Presenting the Small Church," *Tennessee Baptist and Reflector* (17 February 1988), 5.

5. Gary Farley, "The Single-Staff Church and Its Annual Events," *Church Administration* (July 1988), 17.

6. David Ray, *Small Churches Are the Right Size* (New York: The Pilgrim Press, 1982).

Originally published in The Five Stones *(Spring 1997), pp. 15-16; used by permission.*

Chapter 6
THE BIVOCATIONAL OPTION

Stephen Norcross

I believe that God has called me to the ministry of the church. I also believe that God has called me to the practice and professions of teaching and writing. I believe that all these callings are valid, and that it is not essential that I must choose one over the other.

The theme of a meeting of the National Network of Episcopal Clergy Associations a few years ago had us look at the question, "Ministry—where has it been, where is it now, and where is it going?" While the practice of ministry has always included a population of bivocational clergy, the matter is becoming increasingly prevalent. As more and more small- to medium-sized churches discover that their practice of employing a priest, or other clergy, on a full-time basis is too expensive, the option of employing clergy on a less than full-time basis, if not an initially attractive option, is a live one.

I have been a priest of the Episcopal church for over 30 years. More than half of those years in active ministry have been devoted to serving the church while also engaged in professional education. I have enjoyed over 10 years of effective and sometimes satisfying service in my present work as rector (half-time) of St. Martin's Episcopal Church in Lebanon, Oregon. I will outline here those factors that I think lead to the best part-time arrangements between a pastor and congregation. In addition, I'll point out some pitfalls, most of which I've fallen into at times, that can make the arrangement less than satisfactory.

NEITHER A PART-TIME PRIEST NOR A PART-TIME CHURCH

The most important belief underlying a successful part-time arrangement is based on a notion that should be engraved in stone, or at least incorporated into a congregation's mission statement and letter of agreement: *A part-time arrangement between pastor and congregation does not mean that the person is a part-time pastor, nor that the congregation is a part-time church.*

I could no more be a part-time priest than I am a part-time husband, or part-time father, or part-time musician. An unemployed or retired priest, for example, is no less a priest than an employed one. The character that is bestowed at the sacrament of ordination is not dependent on one's outward situation.

A congregation arranging for the services of a pastor on a part-time basis is no less a congregation than one with a full-time pastor, or one with several pastors on its staff. Now it may appear that such a congregation is less active than the larger congregation, but that is often only a matter of appearance. Furthermore, a small congregation with part-time clergy may have a vital and active ministry of laity surpassing that of the larger, professionally managed church (more on that later).

PART-TIME CAN SERVE THE CHURCH'S MISSION

The use of part-time clergy can enhance, rather than negate, a vital sense of a congregation's mission. Unfortunately, many churches that are contemplating the use of part-time clergy are doing so from positions of loss and weakness rather than strength and potential. The conversation may go something like this: "For many years we have enjoyed the services of a full-time clergyperson. However, the economy in our town has suffered some reversals, and it appears that we can no longer afford the compensation package of a full-time pastor. Therefore, we'll just have to adjust our expectations, and do without much of what we used to enjoy."

This sounds pretty sad. Let's rework this statement to put it in a more hopeful and positive manner: "Though for many years this congregation has enjoyed the arrangement with clergy for full-time service, our circumstances are changing. Now, we can look forward to an enhanced ministry of the people of this church, living out our baptismal covenants in ways that have previously been reserved for the clergy. It's an exciting time for our church, and we look for a member of the clergy who, employed with us part-time, will support our ministries as we grow and stretch into what God is calling us to."

What a difference! The one sees the part-time clergy situation as a liability. The other sees it as potential for mission.

PART-TIME CLERGY ARE SOMETIMES EXPLOITED

It is sometimes feared that clergy in a part-time arrangement will be exploited, expected to provide full-time service for less than full-time pay. This has happened. It is true that, at times, church vestries have offered less than standard compensation packages, with the secret hope that the pastor will work extra hard and bring the church's budget up out of the hole. It is also sadly true that some churches in temporary misfortune have played on the vulnerability of clergy, doing an end-run around standards of compensation.

I believe that we clergy are responsible for our own just treatment. If a pastor is being overworked and/or underpaid, it is probably because he or she has failed to set clear boundaries. Clarity of expectations may be the single most important key to a successful part-time arrangement.

A GOOD LETTER OF AGREEMENT PROTECTS ALL

When the vestry/search committee of St. Martin's Church interviewed me in 1991, we discovered that the operations resource manual of the diocese of Oregon did not address the special concerns of part-time arrangements. We wrote an addendum for my standard letter of agreement:

1. The position shall be known as part-time rector.
2. The rector will be expected to devote half of his professional time to the ministry of St. Martin's Church. A professional work week is understood to occupy about 50 hours. Therefore, the part-time position will normally occupy about 25 hours.
3. Certain seasons require more time. Pastoral emergencies do not wait for certain hours. Therefore, when the rector devotes more time, he is

to take compensatory time off as soon as possible, without additional salary compensation.

4.   The vestry has no authority to define the rector's activities outside of the ministry hours.

5.   The vestry will follow the diocesan guidelines as to financial compensation. They will discover the amount of salary as if the position were full time, and then take a percentage of that to offer to the part-time rector. The vestry may increase this amount if they choose. The rector and vestry will negotiate the salary for the next year by the November meeting of the vestry.

6.   The vestry will provide full medical coverage for the rector and his family, full life insurance coverage (probably through the diocesan policy), and travel allowance, the extent of which will be negotiated by the rector and vestry.

7.   Housing will be provided for the rector and his family, or an allowance in lieu of housing may be provided to the extent allowable by IRS laws.

8.   The vestry is responsible for interpreting to the members of the congregation the status of the part-time rector, constantly reminding them of the partial nature of this position as contrasted with the full-time position.

9.   The vestry is to be assertive in seeing that work formerly done by a full-time rector is done by appropriate laypersons. In addition to administrative duties, such work might include pastoral care, teaching, visiting, and sacramental ministry.

10. The vestry should have clear goals about the part-time position, that is, whether to remain in the part-time position for the future, or whether to reduce or increase the hours of this arrangement.

11. The terms of this agreement will be reviewed annually as part of the mutual ministry review.

The personnel committee of the diocese of Oregon has accepted this document, and has included it in the letter of agreement section of its operations resource manual.

Of particular interest are items 5, 8, 9, and 10. Item 5 requires adherence to the diocesan compensation standard. Item 8 places much of the burden of interpretation to the congregation about part-time work on the vestry. Item 9 underscores the shared ministry of all members of the church, and item 10 reminds the vestry that the part-time arrangement is always open to review and revision.

I am present as many Sundays in the year as I would be if I were full time. I am on-call for pastoral emergencies. In consideration for this "extra duty," my vestry provides me with full housing, and would provide full medical insurance for me and my household should the need be there. Other part-time clergy might be less available, due to commuting circumstances. However the arrangement, it is essential that the clergy and the vestry be very clear about expectations and limitations, especially the potential hardships that those limitations might impose.

POTENTIAL DISAPPOINTMENTS

Bivocational ministry has not been without its difficulties and disappointments. I am not as available for weekday meetings, such as those of our own clergy association, without my attendance costing me time from my other work, and thus costing me some income. Full-time ministry assumes the support of the priest for church matters beyond the parish. My other work makes no such provision.

Part-time clergy are, therefore, often seen to be marginal in the extended church. After a few times of asking my bishop to excuse me from clergy conference meetings and my missing clergy association meetings due to work commitments, it's easy to conclude that I have lost interest. I have one major diocesan responsibility as an elected member of the board of trustees of the Oregon Episcopal School. Since I have other work beyond the church, this is about all I can manage and even that requires quite a bit of planning for the monthly drive to Portland for regular meetings.

I don't mean to suggest that bivocational clergy are necessarily busier or that we put in more total work hours than full-time clergy. What I do mean to suggest is that the time for diocesan meetings and other church-related involvements is built into the work week of the full-time clergy. For bivocational clergy, time must often be begged, borrowed, or stolen from the other job to obtain the time to leave town for such events.

Two part-time jobs sometimes seem to add up to more than one full-time job. I've been fortunate in that my other employers have been flexible when church work, usually a pastoral care situation or holy day service, requires more attention. I'm also fortunate that my vestry and most of my congregation have been very understanding when the other work calls me away from the church for longer periods of time.

Cellular phones and voice mail are mixed blessings for the bivocational (and other) clergy. Sometimes they make my work easier, while at other times I feel pulled in two directions or have no time off. Again, if I am being taken undue advantage of, it's probably because I have failed to set and stick to boundaries.

I've tried moderately hard to return to full-time ministry, and have not been successful. One reason given by a church rejecting me was that by being part-time, I had not demonstrated a recent ability to manage a full-time job. I was angry about that until I had recent reason to serve on the search committee for the principal of our local high school. We rejected several candidates because they were not currently serving schools the same size as ours. I found myself agreeing with their decision. So while it might not be impossible for a part-time clergy to return or move to full-time work in the church, it may be difficult.

THE OTHER JOB?

What kinds of work fit well with a dual-career arrangement? My experience here has been that the two jobs should require approximately the same sets of skills. I've been a hospital chaplain, a preschool administrator, and a classroom teacher. I may wear a clerical collar for the church and a necktie (rarely, since I live in the Pacific Northwest) for the other, and the people are different, but the work is very much the same.

By contrast, I have heard that some dual-career people are happiest when the two works are quite different, requiring contrasting skills. One priest shared her time with the local veterinarian's office, working as a technician. It could, of course, be argued that priest work and vet work involve cleaning up similar messes. She thought the two jobs were different enough that she could shut the door on one and be refreshed by the other. The temperament and preferences of the person in question could point in very different directions.

Growing to Full-Time?

Can a part-time situation grow into full-time? This is an important question, of great interest to both congregation and clergy in a part-time arrangement. As I see it, this is part of a larger question, and a larger observation: Small congregations tend to remain small, while large congregations tend to grow. This in itself is a complex, and controversial, tendency. The reasons behind this are complex, and involve many factors, only one of which is the time arrangement of the priest.

I know of one growing congregation in my diocese that makes use of a half-time rector. Should the growth continue at its present rate, this church will need to negotiate a full-time arrangement with its priest very soon. The priest, however, is working essentially full-time regardless of her financial compensation. The time that she is putting into her work is paying off in increased numbers and increased stewardship.

Part-Stipend Is Not Always Part-Time

Some part-time clergy may choose to give the church more than their financial arrangement would suggest. The church may appreciate this gift greatly. Such an arrangement becomes unjust only if the pastor is involuntarily expected to make such a donation of his or her time and leadership. Church standards of compensation should not be disregarded, however. Regardless of how much actual time the pastor chooses to give, the part-time arrangement between congregation and pastor should be clearly described. It doesn't do the collegiality of the clergy any good for resentments to build because Pastor X is working as hard as Pastor Y for half the salary.

It Can Work!

I've found quite a bit of satisfaction with my part-time work as a priest of this church. This arrangement has given me time to pursue other vocations and avocations. As I compare notes with others in ministry and in other professions, I am very grateful for the gift of time that I might not have in such abundance if I were employed on a full-time basis.

The single most important factor in making it work to everyone's benefit is clarity of expectations and clarity of future goals as derived from a
congregation's mission. Pay attention to these. If the church and its clergy
do so, bivocational ministry can be a very attractive option.

Originally published in Leaven *(June 1999), a publication of The National Network of Episcopal Clergy Associations; used by permission.*

Chapter 7

FOUR MYTHS
ABOUT
BIVOCATIONAL PASTORING

Anthony G. Pappas

When the Midwest Ministerial Leadership Commission of the American Baptist Churches USA asked me to do some research among bivocational pastors, it set me going along what has proven to be an exciting path. The Midwest Commission was convinced that bivocationalism would increasingly characterize the church in the years ahead. They were concerned that there was little in place to help educate and equip persons for such a ministry.

The task they gave me was to interview bivocational pastors who were deemed to have an effective ministry to learn what I could about what was or would have been useful to them in pastoring. In person and by phone, I interviewed about a dozen pastors in four states. Though a very small sample, certain trends began to emerge clearly, one of which disturbed me. It concerned the negative attitude that these faithful, effective bivocational pastors held *toward themselves*. This negative self-image surfaced in the form of four "If only's." I call them myths because in believing them to be true of themselves, these pastors gave these negative attitudes power over themselves and their ministries. I believe that these four attitudes are objectively false, or at most speculative. As with the boy and the emperor in his "new clothes," by naming their clothes as unreal in this article, I hope some bivocational pastors will be helped to see the situation realistically. I hope some will move from self-negating myths to scripts of power and faithfulness.

MYTH #1:
"IF ONLY I HAD GONE TO SEMINARY, I WOULD BE A BETTER PASTOR."

While many bivocational pastors are seminary trained, many, especially in rural areas, are not. They are persons who have taken a "home-grown" path to the pastorate; their callings arose from their faithfulness, gifts, and, yes, needs. Often sensing their limits, "seminary" is elevated in their estimation to somewhere near the New Jerusalem. They believe seminary would overcome all weaknesses of pastoring, fill all voids of knowledge, and compensate for all areas of vulnerability.

Ah, if only it were so! Seminary does a lot of good things. For me, it provided the opportunity to sharpen my theological wits; it was the occasion of meeting dedicated and challenging fellow Christians; and it provided the opportunity to pursue some of my faith issues. I appreciate my seminary experience, but not because it helped me to pastor better. The best I can say is that seminary helped buy me a ticket to on-the-job training! I learned to pastor by pastoring.

Church theologian Tex Sample is not sure that seminary does even that much good. By the time one graduates from seminary, he says, one's left brain is so overdeveloped that one is unfit for pastoring real people! (Real people are his cultural right folk.) Say it ain't so, Tex!

If there is any correlation between effective pastoring and seminary education, it awaits documentation! Maybe what bivocational pastors are saying when they lament their lack of seminary is, "I feel inadequate at certain points in my ministry." Maybe it's okay to feel inadequate given the awesome nature of the pastoral task. Or maybe we can develop equipping exercises that truly enhance effective pastoral behavior. In baseball some of the best trades are the ones that didn't happen. So, too, regarding seminary: Some of the best seminary trainings are the ones that didn't happen.

Myth #2:
"If only I were more committed, I would be a full-time pastor."

Now the "advantages" of full-time pastoring are manifold:

- Full-time pastors seldom experience first hand the stresses and opportunities of secular employment. This doesn't do much for credibility with the laity ("You no playa da game, you no maka da rules!"), but it does a lot to insulate the pastor from (1) temptation and (2) making the faith relevant.
- Full-time pastors can live a wonderfully contradictory life by verbally goading the congregation to greater faithfulness while being the structural bottleneck that ensures the congregation actually does no such thing.
- Full-time pastors can pitch their tents toward the Sodom of "professionalism."
- Full-time pastors can be the "holy one" for the congregation, absolving them from the necessity to perfect their faith.
- Full-time pastors know which side their bread is buttered on. A plane that flies between Block Island and the mainland carries a placard: "There are old pilots and there are bold pilots, but there are no old, bold pilots!" In the same way, there are prophetic pastors and there are full-time pastors, but there are darn few prophetic, full-time pastors.

On the other hand, maybe real commitment is

- giving up evenings and weekends, week in and week out, for the Lord's work
- pastoring a small, poor, low-prestige church that would close under the financial burden of a full-time pastor
- being a mentor of the team of Christians in a local congregation
- acknowledging that God's way of organizing Christ's body for 19 of 20 centuries is without full-time pastors and therefore living in that heritage
- acknowledging: "I can't do it all. Help me. Together we can accomplish God's will for us."

MYTH #3:
"IF ONLY I WERE A GOOD PASTOR,
OUR CHURCH WOULD GROW."

Well, now here's a half-truth or so. True, exceedingly poor pastoring can drive people away. But the converse is not necessarily true: "good" pastoring brings new members. That might be true or not; it depends on three factors:

- *Situational factors*: If Jesus pastored in rural North Dakota, he'd do well to stay even with deaths and out-migration.
- *Congregational factors*: A church utilizing a bivocational pastor often has the form and mentality of a family. For them, "successful" congregational life has the feel of reunion, not enlargement. Good pastoring may enhance growth, but it will be family growth, by birth or adoption, not by mass influx.
- *The redemptive factor*: Once upon a time American culture reinforced the Christian church and vice versa. Today the culture (indulgent, hedonistic, materialistic, and so forth) no longer reinforces the church. Christianity has become a minority religion. Many are now coming to see this smaller position not as failure, but as a start toward success— a reaffirmation of our redemptive role as leaven in society.

MYTH #4:
"IF ONLY I HAD MORE TIME TO GIVE TO PASTORING,
MORE WOULD GET DONE."

Well, maybe. Sometimes more time means less ministry! The clear time constraints of a bivocational pastor are often motivational to the rest of the congregation. If they value it, they'll do it. But let a paid employee enter the scene, and watch how fast everyone backs away! Often the healthiest posture for the whole body of Christ is one of definite limitation—the resource any one person, especially the pastor, can bring.

Time limits can therefore be objectively positive and even the subjective frustration may disguise a positive characteristic. The trying situation of not enough time occurs because of the bivocational pastor's high goals and visions for the kingdom of God. After all, people with no agenda have plenty of time to accomplish it! But those who would see great things done for God get antsy for quicker progress. And, in their eagerness, they focus on what remains to be done instead of what is being done. A small shift in perspective may bring a large change in one's level of fulfillment.

***

Bivocational pastoring is a valid and necessary ministry. If the church is to move forward into God's future, we must find ways to undergird and encourage bivocational pastors. Can we, by placing these four myths on the table and examining them, move our thinking from negation and frustration regarding bivocational ministry to affirmation? We can and we must.

Originally published in The Five Stones *(Spring 1994), pp. 15-16; used by permission.*

Chapter 8

THE SMALL-CHURCH PASTOR:
TOURIST, MISSIONARY, OR ANTHROPOLOGIST?

Anthony G. Pappas

I used to live on a small, seasonal resort island (11 square miles, 700 people) 10 miles out to sea. I liked living there—enough so that I still think of myself as an islander, though I am now only a part-time resident. Well, that is, I liked living there most of the time—say, nine months a year. If the other three months—the summer months—were a painting, Dali would be the artist: They are surrealistic. Every year-round resident is outnumbered 30 to one during the summer (the Alamo stood a better chance!). Police, sewer, water, traffic flow, bank, post office, and patience become strained to the limit. But, mostly, one's sense of reality is put to the test. When you live in a world that is satisfying, meaningful, personal, subject to your power to influence, wholesome, organic, intergenerational, and human scale, it is hard to overhear it being demeaned as "quaint," "charming," "idyllic," and "perfect." No matter how well intentioned, these are not real words to us on the island. And hearing mainland society referred to as "the real world" especially hurts, for I know in my heart that it is an illusion manufactured out of fossil fuels, the Protestant work ethic, and constantly striving egos.

I have always supposed I should like it when tourists act like tourists, but their "oh-ing" and "ah-ing" seems so shallow. Even their sincere questions betray their misunderstanding. When they ask, "What do you do all winter?" we answer, "Knit seaweed," while silently thinking, "What do any people, anytime, anywhere (save in the suburbs of affluence) do but live together and enjoy it?' When they ask, "Do you have electricity?" we answer, "Yeah, but at our pace of life it gets kind of static." But silently we think, "Are we really all that primitive looking—is our Cro-Magnon skull showing through?" When they ask, "Have you lived here all your life?" we answer, "Not yet," while silently thinking, with both arrogance and humility, "Here we live."

The problem with relating to tourists is not with their intention, but with their effect. Fundamentally, every person and every group of people wants to be taken seriously. People on the island are no different. We might chuckle at our foibles, our country bumpkinness, our "characters," but deep down we do not think our way of life is a joke. It is soul satisfying and worthy of respect, not head patting; of esteem, not euphoria. We want to be taken with joyous seriousness. If we are not taken on out own terms, we reject. The tourist is not a valued member of island society.

Of course, tourism is not rejected. The tourist is a valued member of the island economy. Folks here remember all too vividly the impoverishment of being "undiscovered." Because of the tourists our carpenters work, stores stay open, and the church stays in the black. We need the tourist business, but we don't necessarily like it. It is an uneasy coexistence. They are with us, but not of us. We live in relationship with them; we even like many of them. But we don't, can't, give them our hearts.

Some tourists get hooked, though. It dawns on them, in a revelation akin to Paul's on the Damascus road or Newton's under the apple tree, that there are three other seasons on the island, a fact amazingly similar to the rest of the world. These few discover that the island's fall quaintness and spring quaintness far exceed its summer quaintness, and the winter quaintness is positively off the scale. They start coming weekends and holidays year-round. They covet property and build an oversized and conspicuously placed house. And—here is the irony of it all—they think that their sophisticated skills, insights, and abilities are valued in the land of quaintness. In this they are sadly mistaken. It is their energy that is valued (in the equally mistaken notion on the part of islanders that it might protect them against the next batch of missionaries).

Missionaries—that's what these people are. They come to us from a superior culture, emissaries of a new and improved way of life. They come here to make a difference, to change things for the better. The vision of the great society is theirs and, but for some unexpected and incomprehensible intransigence (original sin?) on the part of the natives, they would achieve it. The saving gospel is known to them and they preach it from every committee, financial town meeting, and issue of the newspaper. They preach a coming doom, the need to save ourselves "from this perverse generation," and "Behold, now is the day of salvation." And they speak a language filled with weighty theological terms, such as investment, interface, and infrastructure. All in all, they are strange visitors from another culture, faster than we ever thought of being, more powerful than a bull in a china shop, able to leap to committee chairmanships in a single coup, and who, disguised as one of us, fight a neverending battle for control, efficiency, and the American Way. Regarding these missionaries, we pray that God may save us from them all, or if not that, then please God, convert them.

Most of these missionaries eventually become frustrated with the backward ways of island life, shake the dust off their beach thongs, and sell out at a tidy profit. But some stay. They winterize their houses, sink down roots, retire or pre-retire to the island, and, in general, become quieter and wiser. Island life, island history, island ways, and island people become less the object of change and more material of endless fascination and interest. The terms *inferior*, *backwater*, and *primitive* give way to *different*, *unique*, and *alternative*. Our rural, less hurried, more personal culture starts to be recognized for what it is: ancient, legitimate, and vulnerable. The enterprise of transformation is gradually replaced by the quest for understanding. Acceptance and finally appreciation come to the fore as the island's culture is now embraced simply for itself.

Of course, the island culture is not perfect—far from it, actually—but it is an integrated system distinct from and at variance with mainland, mainstream culture. So, after a while, some missionaries become anthropologists—willing to accept a culture on its own terms with its own uniqueness and legitimacy. Slowly they let go of the lifelines that tied them to other ways of living and allow themselves to slip into the deep waters of a new culture. Not unpredictably, once they relinquish their efforts at kicking and screaming, they find themselves floating, refreshed, and actually enjoying themselves. Not in exactly the same way as those who have adopted them—for the natives know little else—but as those who know two systems from the inside and humbly and gratefully accept this new one with understanding and appreciation.

Yet there is, I believe, a further stage. When respect is accorded it usually is reciprocated. When space is shown to be appreciated, it is usually extended. Those who stand together eventually become one, if only in agreeing to disagree. But the line is crossed, nonetheless. Now we live as family—squabbling and making up, progressing and backtracking. So the anthropologist moves on to become a member, even an elder, of the tribe in a way the tourist and missionary never could. Change can still be worked for, but now it is for mutually agreed-upon goals and with mutually agreeable means, because there is mutuality. They become us. I becomes we.

Identity is no longer lodged in the changes effected but in relationships—in the place accorded within the family. "Your people will be my people and your God my God" (Ruth 1:16). On that basis only did Ruth become a part of salvation history, of God's transforming plan. In the case of the clergy, the missionary becomes the pastor by becoming one with the people. Then he "is respected at the city gate, where he takes his seat among the elders of the land" (Prov. 31:23).

So let us consider the clergy. I have been writing from my experience of how this island community progressively includes new members into its society. But my further intention is to claim that the same progression must be completed if a pastor is to be included in a small church's society. I see in the social dynamics of my small rural community a picture of the social dynamics usually operative within the small church. And I see the need to move through these various roles if a pastor is to have a healthy, productive, and long-term pastorate in the small church. An understanding of the existence and sequence of these roles will, I believe, help pastors to journey through them less clumsily and more rapidly.

The long-suffering, life-long lay member of a small parish is structurally in the same position as a member of the base community in a resort area. They have seen plenty of pastors come and go. Over the years they have become somewhat inured to them. They debate which type is worse: those who value them for the difference in their way of doing things from the normal way (the tourist), or those who, after perceiving the difference, move quickly and energetically to change them (the missionary). Rare is the pastor who stays long enough or has the wisdom to move beyond these initial roles. Thus, the small-church lay member often develops a love/hate relationship with the clergy. They are needed by the congregation and there is always the hope that one, at least, will become one with the congregation, stay a good while, and by that life choice show that he or she values and legitimates the congregation. But it feels like that almost never happens. So the small-church romanticist, hopes high at the arrival of the new pastor, learns quickly and becomes a realist. Need them, relate to them, maybe even like them—but don't give pastors your heart. Yet, the pastor who understands and still cares, and stays long enough, is remembered forever.

It is possible to become that sort of pastor (or nearly so!). It is possible in small-church ministry to go beyond the tourist and missionary and become an anthropologist and then a member or even an elder in the clan. It is possible, but it is doubly hard. The parish does not expect a new pastor to stay and therefore they do not open the way readily. And it is also hard because most pastors are not equipped to make the journey. Young pastors are seldom trained in the "folk ways" and social dynamics of a social system such as is embodied in the small church. Long-term small-church pastorates are rewarded neither economically nor with the attribution of esteem by one's peers, the denomination, or society at large. And theologically, too, we have lost the concept of *life* (as distinct from *professional*) ministry, of pastoring from the inside, of pastoring by being one with one's people, of pastoring by journeying and growing together.

It is possible to become a good small-church pastor, but it is a hard and long journey. Those who realize there is such a journey involved in ministry in the small church, and who persevere in the quest, will find that beyond their frustration lies satisfaction.

Originally published in Action Information *14, no. 2 (March/April 1988): pp. 5-7.*

Part Two
LOVING THE SMALL CHURCH

Chapter 9

RAISING SMALL-CHURCH SELF-ESTEEM: TAKING THE HIGH ROAD

Steven Burt and Hazel Roper

O ur hunch is that raising the esteem of small congregations will top the church's agenda for the next few decades. Why? A host of pressures will continue to mount, including inflation, membership decline, the graying of North America, continuing social change, wholesale population shifts, a general climate more favorable to large than to small, denominational stroking, funding allocated to church-growth projects, and many other issues. If we can raise a small church's esteem, however, we can also raise its sights. Low esteem is not an issue by itself; it is not a single ailment with a single cure. There is a multitude of causes and factors. Let's look at a few, keeping in mind that in real church situations the causes are not as easily isolated as they are here for our examination.

CAUSES AND FACTORS OF LOW SELF-ESTEEM

In institutions, low esteem that stems from a *single cause* is usually, but not always, temporary. One parish I worked with was driven to its knees trying to please the pastor. The congregation felt that nothing they did was ever good enough. The people complained, "He was always telling us—from the pulpit, no less—that we were too small, too poor, too selfish, too lacking in commitment. Thank God he left. Thank God!" The next pastor was very loving and affirming, and the church began to thrive. For the most part, the low esteem persisted as long as the pastor's unprofitable service.

Multiple factors can pummel esteem. Often a complex problem is mistakenly perceived as having a single cause. One example is an outdated or deteriorating facility, such as the 1950s white elephant the present congregation inherited. However, a declining membership and a dwindling support base compound the basic problem of the building. The congregation grays; more and more of the folks live on fixed retirement incomes. Utility costs soar, especially heating fuel. Plumbing and wiring may need major work. Add to that the subtle and unnoticed changes in the congregation's needs: Present membership requires handicapped access, a sound system for the hearing impaired, and a health department code-approved kitchen. Throw in the cost of tuning that old pipe organ and—whew! But like single-factor low esteem, multiple-factor low esteem may disappear with the completion of a new facility or a major renovation project.

Tremendous damage results from *mistaking symptoms for causes*. Not long ago I received a church newsletter that described a congregation's cash shortage. Their pastoral salary costs had risen steadily while most of their aging membership struggled to survive on fixed incomes, or died. Yet I knew they had always been committed people who gave until it hurt in support of their church. Because there was not enough to pay all the salaries, operating expenses, denominational askings, and benevolences, the pastor and finance chairperson relentlessly printed "red ink" notices in the newsletter and weekly worship bulletin. The pastor's letter said, "If we were *more committed* [italics mine], we wouldn't have this financial problem." That pastor had mistaken a *symptom*—cash shortage—for a cause—lack of commitment. Actually, the congregation was devoted and they deserved to be told that. Without acknowledging and affirming their commitment, the church's esteem would be severely damaged. Congregational esteem might be improved by hiring a different pastor, or at least by the current pastor changing his attitude and behavior. Yet the primary issue probably is not the pastoral leadership. Instead, it is the factors stemming from the church's changed financial and membership base that should be scrutinized.

The pastor of a 200-member church near New York City told me the congregation faced the hardest financial crunch and membership decline in its 25-year history. At the urging of this loving and capable pastor, they considered a shared-minister arrangement with a nearby church of similar size experiencing the same difficulties. Folks at that church submitted to the plan; in their resignation, they spoke from their heads and not from their hearts. Their rationalization was convincing, but their voices told another story. They sounded glum, depressed, and spiritless.

"If we don't yoke with the other church, we've got to close our doors," they told me. Yet when I asked them about their financial problems, nearly everyone said, "Things are tight, but we've been in these situations before and have come through it. But the pastor insists things are desperate and we've got to yoke as soon as possible if we're to save this church."

In short, the pastor had *misinterpreted* the signs. Yes, there *was* a cash flow problem and the denominational askings were behind for several years. "Look, we still managed to pay two-thirds last year and three-quarters this year," the treasurer said proudly. Yes, there was a noticeable membership decline—a couple of key families had left the area and two other active couples approached retirement. Unfortunately, several esteem-boosting factors were overlooked because of the "four M" focus on institutional survival: money, members, mortar, and maintenance.

First, *sharing a pastor or closing the doors were not the only two options.* The people jumped too quickly in their decision to share a pastor. Many churches mistakenly believe that being a full-time church means employing a full-time minister. One solid option is employing a part-time staff to tackle a temporarily difficult situation. This solution was never considered, though it should have been.

Second, *the strength of the congregation was sorely underestimated.* The congregation demonstrated a positive track record spanning 25 years. The church was trying hard, a fact that was overlooked. The pastor, not wanting to disappoint the denominational supervisors, saw the payments from a different perspective than the church treasurer saw them. The pastor emphasized the shortage: in his estimation, the church's cup was one-third empty.

Third, *new members were coming in.* Young people with children were attracted to the pastor, the congregation, and the programs. The visitor-turned-member ratio was amazing, with newcomers attending from a 20-mile radius beyond the old surrounding neighborhood. However, this statistic was missed.

Talk about misreading the signs! This congregation was not sliding downhill; instead, it was entering a cycle of renewal. It would have been a huge mistake to share a pastor with another congregation of the same size. Losing *that particular pastor*—one of the keys to that parish's renewal—would have been terrible.

The people pointed out that the pastor, even though acting out of love and concern, had created a congregational *faith crisis*. They objected, "Don't you have faith in us? Do we have faith in our membership? Doesn't our track record indicate we're trying? Can we have faith in you as our leader, or will you bail out when things get tough?" The pastor realized he had pushed the panic button. He repented and publicly asked the congregation's forgiveness, and a healthy pastor-parish relationship was restored.

By uplifting the congregation's strengths and clarifying issues, church esteem turned upward and the people soared on eagles' wings. Two years later the same pastor was still in place, many improvements had been made, programming was stronger, bills were paid, mission and outreach increased higher than ever, and the church was awaiting the arrival of a new steeple.

There is a strange paradox I have discovered about small churches. The people think they do not try hard enough when in fact many try *too* hard. They strain to compete according to the models of a different size organism or large church. It is not uncommon for family- and pastoral-size churches to adopt a program-size church approach to activities. They do so for several reasons. Perhaps the incoming pastor is inclined that way and "feels" program-sized behavior is the way to be a good church. Perhaps newer members enter from program church backgrounds and bring those expectations. Then there is the dominant culture's obsession with competition. This approach frequently leads to burnout, a sense of failure, and low church esteem. Many small churches struggle to fulfill impossible expectations, especially in establishing programs. The people weary. Down on themselves, they minimize their natural strengths and maximize their weaknesses. A small congregation that overexerts itself often accomplishes nothing but frustration.

My advice? Do not strive, particularly if you play someone else's game according to their rules. Do not try to be someone else. Be yourself, and be comfortable with the church God has called you to be. Pick or design those programs that are right for your specific context and that will best use your congregation's gifts and talents. Be unique and different part of the time; other times, borrow ideas from other churches if these will work for you. Try what one pastor calls "cheap thrills"—programs that are high visibility with low energy drain. Publicize, celebrate, and offer visible appreciation.

Keep in mind that the following ideas may be morale boosters that generate temporary positive esteem. This may be all that some churches need at the time. "Cheap thrills" programs are not meant to replace important needs, such as tackling the church's self-esteem. Understandably, serious issues will require more time and specialized assistance.

Eight Ways to Take a Programmatic Approach without Being a Program Church

1.   An 83-member New York church has an average attendance of 25. More than three-quarters of the worshipers are retired, many in their 70s and 80s. The group cannot engage in outreach activities that require high energy, but when they discovered they were photogenic, they came up with a novel idea. Each week after worship the congregation poses before a Polaroid. They then send the photo—along with a card signed by everyone—to a different person selected for the week. They often choose a person who is not a church member. These *Card-'n'-Photos* have been sent to a college student; to the oldest woman in the denomination (age 117); to a high-school scholarship winner; to the local Fireman of the Year; to a 78-year-old Maine woman earning her bachelor's degree; and to the widow of a past minister of the church. They call their endeavor a *ministry of hospitality*. What a suitable project for this particular congregation.

2.   The same congregation felt that putting on regular fund-raising suppers was too strenuous for most members. They decided they could manage at least one special supper each year. They hosted a Volunteer Fire Department *appreciation banquet* for the local 80-member fire company and auxiliary—the first in its 100-year history. Decorations were creative, speeches were short, and the pot roast was delicious. These two ideas were simple, appropriate, highly visible activities that helped the church feel good about itself.

3.   A 240-member Vermont church collects food for the local emergency food pantry by hosting a *Shopping Bag Sunday*. Two Sundays in advance, each worshiper is handed a brown paper shopping bag on the way out of worship. Each bag has stapled to it a list of the most-needed items for the food shelf. People are asked to return them—filled with food—on Shopping Bag Sunday. The bags are carried to the altar during the first hymn; there is a powerful, visible impact on the worshipers, especially on the visitors. They see faith put into action.

4.   The same church celebrates World Communion Sunday each year with a *Bread Fest*. Worshipers are asked to bring a loaf of their favorite

homemade bread or their favorite spreads. What a tasty assortment of breads ranging from zucchini, carrot, pumpkin, to cranberry, topped with homemade or store-bought jams and jellies! After a brief service in the sanctuary, everyone proceeds to the fellowship hall for the communion service. One of the donated loaves is used for the Lord's Supper; afterwards everyone samples the many breads and spreads. For several years World Communion Bread Fest and Shopping Bag Sunday were combined. The food went to stock the local pantry; the leftover breads were delivered to the soup kitchen, and a special offering was forwarded to a denominational mission. These activities are highly visible, contextually appropriate, produce high value with minimal energy investment, and boost esteem tremendously.

5. A Massachusetts church collected new and used *jigsaw puzzles* to be used by a cancer treatment center. The puzzles were placed on a table in the waiting room so patients awaiting treatment could work alone or together to pass the time. The project has high value for low energy output.

6. Many churches have discovered the value of *pew Bibles*. Worshipers can read the morning scripture together, silently or aloud. Just buying the Bibles can be a worthwhile way to raise congregational self-esteem. The American Bible Society sells hardcover pew Bibles in many versions for a nominal cost. Asking members to purchase one or more Bibles is a simple way to cover costs. Each copy can be dedicated in memory or in honor of someone by using glue-in bookplates. A special dedication service is appropriate.

7. Another church set up a *mission and outreach tree*, a terrific visual aid that raised awareness and esteem. Someone found a plywood tree that had been used as a sign for the annual Christmas bazaar. People created leaves that were placed on the tree with thumbtacks, with each leaf describing a mission or outreach of the church. Once those leaves began covering the tree, everyone was amazed at how much the church was doing without their realization. People added even more leaves to the tree, noting that the congregation had three people on the five-person local school board and citing the number of its members on the boards of nonprofit agencies. Both of these are noteworthy examples of God's service.

8. Another church recognized that many people could not afford a Palm Sunday ham dinner, a tradition shared by many of the parishioners. So the church sponsored a *Hams-for-the-Haven Palm Sunday food drive* (The Haven is the local shelter which also dispenses emergency food and holiday baskets to the needy). During Lent, the season of sacrifice, worshipers were reminded to buy a canned ham to bring on Palm Sunday. During the offertory worshipers were asked to bring the hams and their regular morning offerings to the altar. The congregation, which averaged 60 worshipers, had 90 folks in attendance that day. The food offering was generous: 62 hams were left at the altar.

There are countless projects that bring congregations together without overtaxing resources. Many of these are simple and fun, and at the same time raise small-church esteem. Try a community walk to fight hunger or a blanket Sunday to fight the cold. Or send much-needed used clothing to one of the Appalachian missions your denomination supports. Have a silly awards night at church, recognizing behind-the-scenes workers (what I call Holy Hoopla). Get a printer to run off a community birthday and anniversary calendar. Support a missionary or a seminarian.

If low or mediocre esteem is an issue for your church:

- *Do not judge* your church by another congregation's standards for success
- *Do not jump to conclusions*, mistaking symptoms for causes; beware of faulty perceptions
- *Do not try too hard*; maybe it is easier than you think
- *Be unique*, but borrow ideas that work
- *Test out* a few high visibility ideas that do not drain energy ("cheap thrills"); keep the projects simple, easy, and context appropriate
- *Celebrate*, appreciate, make visible
- *Pat yourselves on the back* more often
- *Have fun!*

Although the program approach is not a complete strategy for raising small-church esteem, it can be part of a coordinated strategy. At first glance it may seem to be cosmetic, but it can boost morale leading to an examination of the root causes of low esteem. It must be noted that if a small church in its unique context continually engages in the wrong programs, the consequence will be low esteem.

Questions for Consideration

1. List your church's various program ideas.
2. Which ideas are size and context appropriate?
3. Which programs seem difficult to accomplish or are frustrating?
4. Which are stale ideas from a previous time or from a previous pastor's tenure? Are there ticklish feelings associated with evaluating them and possibly discontinuing them? How do you deal with those conflicting feelings and opinions?
5. Which program ideas are the most fun and which are the most satisfying?
6. What new idea was tried? Did it take hold?
7. How do you pat yourselves on the back, recognize, celebrate, and appreciate?
8. What are the forums that give all a chance to introduce and toss around new ideas without prejudgment? How can the church ensure the continuity of such forums?
9. Brainstorm ideas from other churches, organizations, and places. Which ones might work in your church?
10. What might be some cheap thrill (high visibility/low energy drain) ideas for your congregation to try, to succeed at, and to celebrate as a way of raising esteem and morale?
11. How are programs evaluated after they have been tried? How does the church decide to discontinue programs? Who decides and by what process?
12. What skills and talents are already present in our church that might be utilized in featured programs or in mission and outreach? (During the monthly fellowship time following worship, can someone take and record blood pressures? Can the cooks each contribute a crockpot of homemade soup for a "soupathon"?)
13. What would happen if the church encouraged everyone to work in teams or small covenant groups for a year, with each group seeking a way to use their gifts to design a mission and outreach program?

Originally published in Action Information *18, no. 4 (July/August 1992): pp. 13-16.*

Chapter 10

FEW MEMBERS, MANY GIFTS

Loren B. Mead

Several years ago, while working with some colleagues in several dozen local churches from an array of denominations, exchanging views with lay people and clergy, I became aware of some of the things that are going on in small-membership congregations. Some of these things are pretty obvious, though they're not discussed very often.

This led me to think more about what I call the special gifts of the smaller-membership congregations, gifts I think they have to give to the larger church, but ones that smaller churches need to develop and explore more fully. And the rest of the church needs to be open enough to hear the message. I think of eight gifts.

1. Success in Ministry

I think it's possible that the smaller congregations have an opportunity to develop some guidelines about what it means to be in ministry, and to be successful in ministry. It is quite clear that most of those congregations will not ever fit the criteria for success established by denominations: they probably won't grow significantly in numbers, they probably will stay even or just slightly ahead of inflation in stewardship, they will frequently have years when they have a net loss of membership, they will never erect the majestic buildings that larger congregations can boast. Yet as a congregation of people they have the possibility of doing a splendid job.

As I see the rest of the church, it is often caught up in standards of success that relate to institutional viability, not faithfulness in ministry. The rest of the church badly needs congregations that model and communicate some standards for success in ministry which transcend those things we've come to see as marks of institutional success. Small churches have the potential to offer that gift to the rest of us.

2. Support and Care for Lay Leaders

Congregations with small memberships sometimes do very well in their support and care for lay leaders. Lay leaders in smaller-membership congregations frequently have to serve for long terms. I remember that in the first congregation I served, the church treasurer had held the job for 40 years, the church school superintendent for 35 years. The smaller-membership congregations have sometimes learned to provide the kind of support and encouragement for leaders to take on tasks for the long haul. Larger congregations frequently burn out lay leaders in a much shorter time. What can the larger congregation learn from those that are smaller?

3. Clergy-Laity Cooperation

Smaller congregations can model *new ways for clergy and laity to work together*. A lot of small-membership congregations are just barely able to afford a full-time pastor. Sometimes the loss of one pledger can flip the congregation into an inability to pay the judicatory minimum salary. The first congregation I served could afford a full-time pastor about three years out of four; if the young minister didn't stay too long, a year of "vacant pulpit" could allow the church to restore its treasury. Many small-membership congregations are experimenting with different ways for clergy and laity to share the jobs that must be done to support a local church. The rest of the church needs to learn from them. Even where full-time pastoral leadership is possible, both laity and clergy need creative new ways to share responsibility. Churches with few members have something to teach us about this.

4. Models of Community

In small congregations, sometimes more so than in larger ones, the membership of the congregation is quite diverse. All the people in the community who are related to that denomination come to that one church. In larger towns and larger churches, many congregations have a more homogeneous membership. Smaller congregations can teach us something about how it's possible for diverse kinds of people from all walks of life to live together, work together, and worship together. The larger congregations and the larger church need to look to small congregations for new models of how to be together in community.

5. MINISTRY IN EVERYDAY WORK

In smaller congregations in smaller communities it is often more clearly evident that the people who worship together on a Sunday morning are in ministry the rest of the week as they interrelate with one another in the community. They know each other as schoolteachers, laborers, retired persons, housewives, clerks, and all the other kinds of callings that make up the life of a small town. Such work is not seen under the heading of "lay ministry," but just doing what you ought to be doing as a Christian, living out your everyday calling from God. Congregations in such communities have the possibility of teaching the rest of us a lot about what it means to be in ministry in ordinary day-to-day activities.

6. DENOMINATIONAL CONNECTIONS

Small-membership congregations have special insight into denominational connectedness. Much of the relationship between congregations and the denomination involves unhealthy kinds of dependence or counterdependence. Whether the denomination's polity affirms connectionalism or congregationalism, the reality tends to be the same—that there is a relationship between the local church and the denomination, a need for one another, and a flow of resources one way or the other. The smaller congregation lives on the uncomfortable edge of relationship to the denomination. Frequently it is in the position of being a recipient of funds or help or support. If such congregations can work out ways of mutual accountability and mutual responsibility reflecting an adult relationship, they will have a lot to teach the rest of the church. Denominations do have resources for congregations, and congregations have resources for denominations, resources that transcend the flow of dollars. The frontier between local church and judicatory is one smaller congregations are aware of all the time. They are more likely to discover how to live creatively on that frontier than the rest of us, and we need to learn from them.

7. Dealing with Membership Losses

Congregations with few members have a lot to teach congregations that face significant loss of membership. I think particularly of enormous downtown churches in changing neighborhoods whose membership is dwindling. We might create coalitions between smaller congregations and those great congregations that have fallen on lean times. Some of the crises that smaller-membership churches have lived with for years are brand new to some of our urban churches. There are lessons to be learned.

8. Effective Leadership

One of the greatest gifts that small congregations have to give is effective Christians. Many of the denominational bodies, as well as the city and suburban churches, are deeply indebted to the leadership they have received from members whose early nurture in the faith was carried out in small congregations. Everywhere I go across the country, I find leadership in larger institutions of the church disproportionately borne by those who were nurtured in small congregations. Frequently the smaller-membership congregation is not even aware of the power of this exporting of resources, and almost never is the larger church aware of it. The fact remains, however, that smaller congregations produce a large share of the key lay persons and clergy who lead our denominations. I know of congregations of 30 to 40 members that have in several generations produced five to eight young people who grew up, left home, and became key figures in churches elsewhere, not always of the same denomination. These are extraordinary gifts.

***

I am not convinced by some of the rhetoric about small-membership congregations. I do not believe that "small is beautiful." At least not inevitably.

Small can be beautiful and is beautiful in some situations, but within the church small also means underfunded, weary, feeling like a failure, talked down to.

My experience of "small" is that it is some very difficult things. But we need to remember that those in smaller membership congregations do have enormous gifts to give to the rest of the church. I want to see those congregations focus on enhancing those special gifts and making them available to the church. The church needs those gifts, and it is unlikely that larger congregations will ever develop them if the smaller congregations do not. In spite of the difficulty of their calling, it is a high one.

Originally published in Action Information *9, no. 3 (May/June 1983): pp. 1-3.*

Chapter 11

THE ADVANTAGES AND DISADVANTAGES
OF BEING A SMALLER-MEMBERSHIP CHURCH

Gary E. Farley

> *The Lord remembers us and will bless us:*
> *He will bless the house of Israel,*
>   *he will bless the house of Aaron,*
>   *he will bless those who fear the Lord—*
>   *small and great alike.*

(Psalm 115:12-13, NIV)

A mong the battles I waged while serving as a leader of the town and
country church program for the Southern Baptist Convention was the
tendency for many to transfer the secular American view that "bigger is
better" into their understanding of the mission and work of the churches (a
related battle swirled around the assumption that metropolitan is innately
superior to the rural). The clear teaching of the scripture cited above is that
size neither determines nor indicates God's blessing. Certainly, a church
may be small because it is not doing what God wills for it to do, but it may be
small primarily because it is being faithful in a context or climate where
small is natural. Or it may be small because that is the appropriate form for
the ministry it has been commissioned to perform. On the other hand, a very
unfaithful congregation may draw a big crowd, at least for a time. Therefore, one must use criteria other than size to determine whether or not a
congregation is blessed of God. Personally, I have turned to passages such
as Ephesians 4–6, for a statement of what God expects of churches—unity,
purity, mutual submission, and focused activity. These are the indicators of
health and of blessing.

However, while a small church may be a healthy and a blessed church,
it may have a set of advantages and disadvantages that are, to a large

extent, the result of smallness. I once had occasion to generate a list of these for a conference I conducted with bivocational pastors of small, mostly rural congregations, which I share here for your reflection. As you do, note that often a disadvantage can be turned into an advantage. I will conclude this article with a brief account about how one small church has done just that.

DISADVANTAGES OF BEING A SMALLER-MEMBERSHIP CHURCH

1. Lack of Resources

Often money is tight, trained workers scarce, musicians weak, and maintenance deferred. Often this poverty is exacerbated by comparisons with other congregations that appear to have excess resources. Poor churches, like poor people, may have "poor ways."

2. Absence of Programs/Functions

The various faith families generally agree that there are about five or six basic functions that a church ought to perform—worship, nurture, pastoral ministry, evangelism and outreach, fellowship, and mission support. During the middle of the 20th century, the national agencies of the various American denominational families developed programs that could be utilized in a church to support these functions. For example, Sunday school program materials typically aimed at nurture, with some attention also given to the functions of fellowship and evangelism. For many smaller-membership churches, the lack of participants has resulted in the dropping of some programs with the consequence that certain basic functions have been neglected. In my denomination the national agencies, which are mostly funded by sale of program material, have been slow in responding to this problem, and have not generated a unified curriculum that carefully addresses all of the basic functions. Consequently, not a few of the smaller churches may be failing to address all the functions as they ought.

3. Lack of "Critical Mass"

Some smaller churches have become so small, and so elderly, that their future seems to be in doubt. Their activities are so weak that they do not appear attractive to those they wish to reach and involve in the life of the congregation. For example, they realize that they need to reach young families (or believe that they do), but lacking such families in the first place, they do not seem to be able to attract their targeted group. They sense that they are caught in a vicious cycle, or a downward spiral.

4. A History of Hard Licks

Many smaller congregations have experienced serious conflict and for some it has become episodic. The misbehavior of a pastor or of a lay leader, the mistreatment of a pastor, or harsh gossip about some of the members has resulted in a poor reputation for the church within its community. The scarcity of financial resources has often resulted in conflict between a pastor and the congregational leadership. Overcoming a poor congregational reputation is not easy.

5. Old and Comfortable

Most smaller rural churches have been around for several generations. Some have become comfortable. They have nice facilities; they get along; they do good things; they are respectable and the "family" comes with real regularity. Often these churches have lost sight of the founding vision, however. They have become focused on being and lost sight of becoming, becoming a full expression of what it means to be the body of Christ and extending God's kingdom here on earth.

6. Provincial in Outlook

"We have never done it that way before, pastor." Often, this also implies, "and we had better not do it that way again." Many smaller rural churches have bought into "Fordism," that is, "there is one best way to do things, and that is our way." Certainly, tradition is important. But adherence to it runs the risk of confusing culture and Christianity. Times change. The eternal must be wrapped in the temporal. While care must be exercised not to "throw out the baby with the bath water," the "water" must be disposed of nevertheless. There seems to be an inevitable tension here. It should be dealt with honestly and sympathetically.

7. Pessimistic about People Changing

It seems that with age also comes a degree of pessimism. A heritage of dashed hopes is a part of the baggage carried by the elders of the older, smaller church. Consequently, they have a tendency to pour cold water on the dreams of the youth, particularly of youthful pastors. They recall trying "something like that" and it did not work. They recall personal repentance and conversions that did not last. So, they may be slow about rejoicing at the coming of a convert.

8. Loving Too Much

Usually when one thinks about the advantages of the smaller congregation, the quality of its caring for one another is ranked near the top. Indeed, in a busy, often faceless society, being loved is greatly valued. However, love can smother. An advantage can become a disadvantage. Too often, the small congregation is so busy in its caring for one another that it fails to broaden its circle to include the new people who might want and need to join the circle.

9. Bearing Guilt

Being a bivocational pastor carries with it the probability of experiencing significant levels of guilt. Usually, there is not enough time to do work at the level one wishes to achieve on the job and in the pastorate. Laid on top of this is the fact that often the pastor's family sees itself as short changed as the bivocational pastor attempts to balance the demands and expectations of the job and of the church. When bad things come on the job, in the church

or in the family—as they will—the pastor will tend to second-guess himself
or herself and wonder if he or she failed to manage time correctly.

10. Being Second Class

Both the pastor and the church are often made to feel like failures. If each
had only worked harder or been more faithful, the church would have grown
at least to mid-sized. Like Job's friends, folk seek to find the source of
smallness in some personal or corporate flaw. Pastors in my tradition tend
to respond to this in one of three ways—by being obnoxious, loud, and
critical of their church; being far too humble about being "just a little county
preacher"; or by distancing themselves from fellowship with their pastoral
colleagues. Likewise, the church may become overly proud of its spirituality, which has caused it to be neglected by secular people, perceive itself to
be inferior and insignificant, or distance itself from interchurch fellowship.

***

Certainly, this is not a full listing of the disadvantages of being a small church.
You can probably identify several more. But I hope that this list is inclusive
enough to dispel any saccharine sentimentality about smaller, rural churches.
Actually, while many of these churches are truly wonderful, others are
simply terrible. Further, I hope that this list helps you to be more aware that
there is often a kind of dialectic relationship between disadvantages and
advantages. Like some sin, the problem may lie in the degree. This will
become more evident as I move to a discussion of the advantages.

ADVANTAGES OF BEING A SMALLER-MEMBERSHIP CHURCH

1. Dependence upon God

When a church lacks resources and knows that it does, then it is more likely
to recognize its utter dependence upon God. When you have about all of the
resources that you need, it is awfully easy to cruise along on your own.
When a church is well resourced, it may not be driven to ask tough questions about what the special will of God is for it and its ministry. Those of us

who have pastored limited-resource churches have a better understanding of God's miracles because we have experienced them in the many ways God blesses our little congregation to do great, significant things in the life of the church and its community.

2. Biblical Faithfulness

The picture of church life that one finds in the New Testament is one of close, multibonded relationship. The members saw one another and broke bread with each other daily. I contrast this with the typical suburban megachurch where most of the members may not see each other from Sunday to Sunday. It seems to me that the small rural church, where the members live and families are intertwined, provides a setting in which the rich body-life of the early church can be most nearly duplicated. The fact of multibondedness opens up opportunities for truly struggling over how to live out the teachings of Jesus in everyday life with people who know us very well, people whom we cannot fool, people who have memory of our past acts and with whom we expect have to interact with again and again in the future. The focus must be upon relationship. In such a continuing stream of interactions justice, mercy, faithfulness, and love take on deeper meaning. Certainly, small rural churches and their members are subject to sinning, but the webs of their relationships seem to fit the life situation described in the early church. The teachings of Jesus reflect the activity that characterizes traditional rural communities.

3. The Bible Addresses Rural People

Many of the accounts found in the Bible speak of crops, livestock, wild creatures, rain, sowing, and gathering. It champions the people of the land in the face of their exploitation by the moneyed class and by the nobility. So, the pastor of a rural church finds a ready link between the congregation and the teachings of scripture. Think for a minute about how different it would be to preach a sermon on the parable of the soils in a city church, compared to doing the same in a church that serves a farm community. Or the vine analogy in John 15. Or the passage from the Sermon on the Mount concerning the lilies of the field.

4. Life-Focused Sermons

Have you ever thought about the frustration of a pastor who must seek to bring a word from God to an audience of 5,000, most of whom he does not really know, and most of whom do not know one another? How different this is than the challenge of small-church pastors who know the joys and hurts of each member of their congregations, who think about these things as they seek to prepare their messages, and who, consequently, can enter the pulpit with a sense of assurance that God's Holy Spirit has given them a word that will address a very real need. It is my observation that many rural pastors preach great sermons, and this is the reason. They know their people. They know their needs. Thus, they can bring to them a strong message, an appropriate message from God's Word. Talk about being relevant—it is happening!

5. Heightened Responsibility and Accountability

One cannot hide in a smaller rural church. One cannot live a double life, at least not for long. The heritage of many rural American congregations is in pietism and the Great Awakenings. These events and movements called for accountability. Providing nurture for one another and the acceptance of spiritual criticism from a fellow church member were significant elements of the church member in this heritage. While the practice of "church discipline" which gave expression to this last century has fallen into disuse in this one, the foundational concept is still present. Believers ought to be different. They ought to be actively involved in the ministry of the church. They must hold one another accountable for moral behavior that measures up to the teachings of Jesus.

6. Knowing One Another's Spiritual Gifts

Congregations seem to be gifted for the ministries God wants it to provide. It is the task of the church to recognize and evoke those gifts in the life of its members for the ministry of the church. It is a wonderful sight to see a congregation busy with ministry as the members exercise their gifts.

7. High Touch

If you have ever needed the ministry of a smaller rural congregation, and it happened, you will connect with this concept. It is so comforting, so empowering to know that this wonderful congregation really cares about you and your hurts, your joys. Often it seems to spring out of an attitude on the part of those who minister—I have been blessed; I have been forgiven; I have been the object of caring ministry, now it is my turn. The love of God is made manifest in the touch of these congregations.

8. Signature Ministry

Often the smaller rural church does not have the resources, or the need to do the full "menu" of programs provided by its denomination. So, rather than wear itself out trying to live up to the expectations from "headquarters," it has zeroed in, and is specializing on one or two or three activities that it can do well. Unlike the very large (and even most mid-sized) congregations, it does not try to be a "full-service" church. No, it focuses on those things that need to be done in its area which it seems gifted to do. This becomes its signature ministry, the one it is famous for in its region. It draws folk who want to perform that ministry and those who need it. This congregation comes to see itself as a part of a church ecosystem, as a part of the spreading kingdom of God. It has its ministry, which compliments the ministry of other churches in the region, and which in turn is complimented by theirs.

9. Connecting

God has called some very gifted persons into bivocational ministry to serve these smaller rural churches. They bring to ministry some unusual gifts that God blesses to enrich the church. Often they gather persons to the church from their work setting. Often they find their ministry enhanced by the fact that they know the hurts and joys of their fellow employees; therefore, they preach and teach with unusual realism. Further, some of the unchurched find a ring of reality in the life of bivocational pastors. Not a few times God has blessed in tremendous ways the efforts of bivocationals.

10. Appropriateness

It has been easy for mission strategists and others in this age of glorifying bigness to neglect to see that for some people groups and for some places, small is the appropriate size for a church. Perhaps you have visited Cade's Cove in the Great Smokies National Park. This was an isolated, small community, rich in land quality. Its total population never exceeded 800. A total of four congregations served Cade's Cove. One church would not have been adequate before the advent of the automobile because of distances. Significant theological and social issues made consolidation impossible, so a set of small churches seems to have been most appropriate to serve the needs of a sparsely settled region. This is also true all across the country in many rural places and among many small pockets of peoples who are a minority within their setting.

***

Again, you might be able to add several other important advantages that characterize smaller, rural congregations. It seems to me that God wills to have a very diverse set of worshiping, working congregations. In a dialectical sense each has advantages and disadvantages. This is simply the way life is.

A Case Study

Perhaps you lead a church that abounds in disadvantages. Consider how you might turn these into advantages. I know of a church that was small and troubled 25 years ago. Pastoral tenure was short. It was one of six congregations in the township that it served. Total population was less than 1,000. Attendance ran in the low 30s. There were three other Baptist churches within three miles, a United Methodist congregation, and a Church of the Brethren. The other Baptist churches appealed to blue-collar folk. This church had been founded and built by a major landowner in the area. The building was a beautiful brick structure with handsome stained glass windows. It sat on the bank of a large Tennessee Valley Authority lake.

Change began with the calling of a professor from a nearby college as a bivocational pastor. His style of worship leadership appealed to most of the existing members. He networked with five to 10 of the students at the college who had come from small churches. He asked them to come over and work with the music and youth programs. They reached out to the unchurched in the area. He called upon disgruntled former members and upon new neighbors who had built on or near the lake. He also related well with the children and grandchildren of the founder—people who maintained summer homes in the community, but lived most of the year in Florida. He initiated an outdoor Sunday school that met during the summertime in a nearby campground. He initiated better maintenance and improvements to the church house. He stayed for five years, as has each of his four successors. The church now has 80 to 100 in worship and seems very stable. Most of the leaders from 25 years ago are now dead, but they have been replaced with good, progressive leaders. The impact of the founding family is now much diminished.

Note that this bivocational pastor was able to redirect the efforts of this congregation. He recognized that it was different than the three other Baptist churches in its old parish area. Instead of trying to compete with them for the same set of people, carrying a disadvantage of class differences, he focused on their strengths—an attractive building, progressive and modern worship, and access to a stream of talented young persons to service good programs and events. He broke the short-tenure pattern. He initiated some new ministries. And he expanded the field served by the church from six to 30 miles. Its new reputation became that of a lovely church, in a picturesque setting, with quality worship for the more moderate wing of the Baptist movement.

Certainly, this brief case study glosses over a host of problems and mistakes. But it does illustrate that disadvantages can be made over into advantages by a leader who has a vision and who can gather up a set of supporters who will commit to the vision. Certainly, this cannot be replicated in every small, dysfunctional congregation. But in far more than most imagine positive change can occur.

Originally published in The Five Stones *(Winter 1999), pp. 2-8; used by permission.*

Chapter 12

A Love Letter

to

People in Ordinary-Sized Churches

Caroline A. Westerhoff

I remember the Christmas I first realized the value of the small gift. I was eight or nine years old and still delighted in the large and heavy packages bearing my name. I explored the mysteries around the base of the tree, seeking them out, rattling and guessing.

But that year one package defied my curiosity. It did not reside under the tree; it was on a branch. And it was tiny. I had not asked for anything tiny. I knew the good stuff came in big boxes—the bigger the better. Everybody knows that.

That the tag on this more than modest one bore the names of my uncle and aunt furthered my consternation. I had always liked their gifts to me; they were different from the usual. I felt betrayed by obvious oversight. I rattled and shook my way around the base of the tree, ever casting a disappointed yet curious eye toward the offending box on the branch.

Christmas morning did arrive—as it always does despite the doubts of waiting children. Can you guess which package I opened first? The little box on the branch.

I pulled away the paper surrounding a bright yellow wooden chest. Cascading over it was a hand-painted spray of red and blue flowers. I pried the lid open and to my delight out poured a stream of small dolls, dressed in colorful costumes of Central America. I was entranced. I ignored the bigger packages—for a time anyway. I lined up the dolls in one dance configuration after another. To this day, my inner eye strays to that box on a branch.

In spite—or maybe because—of those formational insights that Christmas, I confess I have difficulty with the adjective *small* (for example, in describing people as members of small churches). Listen to some synonyms for "small" from the *Random House Thesaurus*: little, tiny, undersized, slight; meager, scant, modest, not great; inconsequential, insignificant, trivial, superficial, unimportant, lesser, trifling, of no account; mean, petty, narrow, bigoted, provincial; feeble, weak, fragile, faint.

Now listen to the comparable ones under "large": big, great, grand, immense, spacious, roomy, expansive, imposing; substantial, considerable, ample, goodly, liberal, unstinted, extravagant; comprehensive, extensive, broad, sweeping, far-reaching, unlimited, boundless; mighty, towering; magnificent, stupendous—albeit with the inclusion of the less-than-attractive: heavy, rotund, obese, fat, portly, overgrown, ponderous, and monstrous.

Small is typically judged as relative to something else. Small does not stand on its own; it's not something of value in itself. In the language of our culture, large has more positive connotations, and small, more negative ones. To be small carries inherent limitation. We too often lose sight of the truth brought home to me by those dolls.

It is only natural then that we assume a successful church to be a large church, one with possibility for impressive facilities and an array of programs and activities for its members. Given the limitations of our language and the assumptions of our culture, those of us who are not large can suffer debilitating, paralyzing thoughts and feelings of inferiority. If we can't do it like the large church—the norm against which we are compared—either we don't try, or we see our efforts as second best.

But just suppose that small congregations were normative—the standard against which all churches should be measured? We would no longer label a church "small." What is now called a small church would simply be called church. Churches of a size larger than yours would be considered an anomaly rather than the rule, and qualifying adjectives for them would be necessary.

It is important to make three points. First, we are not suggesting that the issue of size is to replace faithfulness or that external criteria are to replace interior ones. From these perspectives size makes no difference.

Second, we are not speaking against church growth. Jesus calls us to "make disciples of all nations"—to baptize them and to teach. Wrapping our walls tightly around ourselves so that we can be something called church would not constitute being church at all. But we are suggesting that congregations in rapidly growing areas and congregations with many members must work hard at finding ways to be church within the limitations imposed upon them by their size. (Limitations imposed upon *them*. Nice for a change!)

Third, we would be naïve to discount what can be done by congregations with considerable resources at their disposal—work of feeding, housing, teaching, advocating. As we see ourselves bound to them by virtue of our common membership in judicatory, national church, and body of Christ, we gratefully know they do this work in our names as well.

Further, as long as we do not become trapped by the necessity of tailoring the life of the small church to theirs, we can receive clues from them about being more faithful in our own ways. Their efforts can provide windows for our imaginations, for we too are called to feed, to house, to teach, to speak.

And the small church's gift to them? To hold up the picture of what church can and must be—a familial community of faith. Look at the word small again: gentle is also a meaning.

Originally published in Action Information *18, no. 4 (July/August 1992): pp. 17-18.*

Chapter 13

BECAUSE WE ARE A SMALL CHURCH, WE CAN . . .

Melvin G. Williams

When the chair of the board of deacons of a nearby church called, I was not surprised. I knew that his pastor was about to retire and that my name had been suggested as a possible part-time interim. "Because we're a small church—a lot smaller than where you are now—you'll find there are things we can't do," he pointed out. "But I hope you'll come to talk with us anyway."

Following my caller's lead, I found myself thinking about how the new assignment would be different. How much smaller? Under 150 members instead of close to 1,000. A budget under $30,000 instead of several hundred thousand dollars. No full-time staff at all instead of two clergy, a secretary, and a custodian. Later on the rest of the deacons would add their own details: not able to get enough volunteers for standing committees, not able to do many programs, not able to afford a full-time secretary.

There is a lot they could not do. But they wanted me to come, they said, and I was eager to join them while they made preparations to call their first full-time pastor in more than a dozen years.

I thought I knew already the sort of church this would be. A neighborhood church identified for almost a century with the small New England mill community where it stood, a community that, now that the mill had closed, was fast becoming a middle-class bedroom suburb. A century-old building in which the shared memories of five generations joined most persons into an extended family. A church that newcomers chose deliberately over the larger and older congregation of the same denomination in the center of town less than four miles away. A place where worship was informal and comfortable. The kind of church someone has described as "more a center of belonging than of believing."

I looked forward to the range of things this small church could do precisely because it was small. And I hoped to learn answers to a head full of questions. I was not disappointed.

- *Because it was small, members could know one another.* But would that assure intimacy for everyone or guarantee the welcome of new-comers?
- *Because it was small, members could care for one another.* But would they also care for those out of sight and perhaps also out of mind?
- *Because it was small, adult members could learn together.* But with only one study group at a time, could we reach persons uninterested in our particular mini-courses or unavailable when we met?

Becoming their interim pastor took some adjusting on my part. To be-gin with, none of my churches had ever been this small. Also, by training and experience I have been a college professor for most of my professional life, in addition to being an interim pastor. I am often rational, task oriented, and orderly. That part is sometimes in tension with the rest of me that is committed to relationships—emotional, spontaneous, closer to people than to program. I combine the two parts—the being part with the doing part—by being scheduled yet relaxed.

Would I be the right "fit" for this church? Certainly that was not auto-matic. Yet I knew that I had not only much to learn but much to give. I was eager to begin. I wanted to test my insights in several ways, and the chances came throughout my 14 months there.

At one point, I remember, some of the deacons had been talking about inclusive language, and I pointed out that a revision of our United Church of Christ Statement of Faith had been specifically prepared as an inclusive language document. A few persons had read it already, and they all agreed that it should be examined by the entire diaconate and by the church council.

There was considerable discussion. Most persons supported the idea of inclusive language, but they were also concerned that to do so in this case would exclude the significant historical language of "Father" for God. [The second version replaces "We believe in God, the Father of Jesus and our father" with "We believe in God, the Eternal Spirit."] The key to the decision came in the observation by the oldest and most honored person there. "I don't think we could go wrong if we used the language Jesus did," he said. "I don't remember that he discriminated against anyone."

The patriarch had spoken . . . gently but clearly. That was not the time for linguistic analysis. The proposed change was defeated, and God remained "the Father of Jesus and our father."

Again, for a second time, tradition prevailed, and I found it interesting to see how it could be brought to bear on a current task. The adult forum, with a high attendance and an even higher enthusiasm, had been meeting each Sunday before worship. Building on the interest generated by the inclusive language issue, we had begun to discuss church creeds in a mini-course titled "We Believe." Its goal was to develop an accurate statement of faith for this congregation, expressing their own beliefs in the light of what had been written years before in the historic creeds.

Week after week that study went well, especially well. As I sought to account for its success, I reviewed the dynamics of the interim period in which a church not only looks to its future but also comes to terms with its unique past. But there was more to it than that. Only later did I learn that the search committee for the new permanent pastor had requested study on that theme as a way for the congregation to think through their beliefs. Yes, they were looking ahead . . . but in the process they were also carefully checking the prescription of the old lenses through which they looked at themselves, their faith, and their mission.

Several members of the study group asked me to choose the next topic—something, they said, they probably wouldn't have chosen themselves. That seemed like a refreshing challenge, and one that could displace the inward-looking characteristic of the small church. So I proposed a series on poverty, as both a theological and a practical issue, to be titled "But the Greatest of These Is Justice." Poverty was a national priority of my denomination and a major concern in a state that boasts one of the highest per capita incomes in the United States yet is home to two of the nation's poorest cities.

We looked at the realities of poverty in Hartford, the capital city only 20 minutes away, using multimedia materials developed at Hartford Seminary. We learned about bridge programs that linked inner-city congregations with the suburbs and rural towns not far off. But while there was some interest, there was little involvement. The discussions, when there were any, almost always came back to their own middle-class world: white, middle-class, and small-town, into which poor persons from other places occasionally came.

Unexpectedly, I learned how they responded to poverty when a middle-aged woman came into the building after worship one wintry Sunday, wearing only a sweater over her slip and nothing else except worn shoes. She wanted gas money, she said, "to help us get on our way." Stopped at the curb outside we found her husband, who explained that he'd stayed in the old car "to keep the engine running. If it dies it'll probably stay dead forever. Besides," he added, pointing toward the pile of blankets in the back. "I don't want the cat to get loose."

Some of the deacons asked them to stay awhile, offered to find them a place to spend the night, even promised to go with them to the unemployment and welfare offices in the morning. But the couple preferred a full tank of gas instead at the station around the corner, plus some sandwiches and coffee for the road. We never saw them again.

Afterward, members talked about the couple with deep concern. "I wish they'd have let us do more," one said, adding that she was "glad at least that they knew to come here for help." Meanwhile, attendance in the study group continued to dwindle.

Do I have concerns about the small church—about this one, at least? Yes, and all are related to the people's need to reach beyond themselves.

It was often difficult for the church to truly affirm diversity, and sometimes it even appeared to be homogenized or segregated. One life member, for instance, described a retired "newcomer" as "becoming involved too soon" because he agreed to become the treasurer after he'd been a member for only two years! Another man, learning that the abandoned mill a few hundred yards away might become a block of condominiums, worried that the new neighbors and potential members wouldn't be "our kind of people." In a larger sense, such a small church may find it easier to gather around one another than to gather for mission. What develops may be a church whose people seek comfort before service and a pastor who is a chaplain instead of a prophet, a church that is happy with the status quo.

But then I thought regrettably, this description suits many larger churches as well.

What worked best in this small church? Almost always, relationships: Delighting in a widow's story of her marriage 63 years before in the parsonage. Grieving over broken confidences. Celebrating weddings. Cooking corned beef and cabbage in a crowded kitchen. Encouraging the young people who planned to be confirmed. Praying and hoping during surgery. Singing joyfully on Christmas Eve. Hugging one another's youngsters on Sunday mornings. Hugging my wife and me too.

Yes, of course there are things a small church cannot do. But this congregation has called its new pastor, the first woman to serve the church in more than 100 years. Pledges have more than doubled in two years. In a major mission project the congregation has purchased a heifer, which is being raised on a member's farm until it is ready to ship to a needy family.

Now people have begun to talk about things they can do . . . because they are small.

Originally published in Congregations: The Alban Journal *19, no. 6 (November/December 1993): pp. 8-9.*

Chapter 14

SMALL CHURCHES, FAITHFUL REMNANTS

Steven Burt

I n his wonderful book *Blue Highways*, about seeing America by way of the back roads, author William Least Heat Moon writes a line I love: "Life doesn't happen along the interstates. It's against the law."[1] The people in the small churches I work with find that their spirits resonate to that statement.

And yet our American culture of the 1980s and 1990s tells us that life and its fulfillments are to be found not in the rural or the small, but in the fast track, in the cities, in the sports cars zipping in and out of traffic on the freeways. A myth has been propagated for years now that bigger is better: the large economy size means a better deal and you're smarter for making that choice even if you don't need that much; the best thing in life is to coast through it securely by hooking up with a huge organization that offers the best pension and benefits; and on and on.

Unfortunately we often receive—intended or not—similar messages from our various denominational front offices. Panicked by statistics indicating wholesale institutional decline (meaning finances and membership), the frenzied bureaucratic voices cry, "Evangelism. Church Growth. Numbers. Sign-'em-up. Reel-'em-in!"

With all these voices in the marketplace crying out, each espousing its particular "Life-giving gospel," we in the rural and small churches find ourselves resonating to a line like, "Life doesn't happen along the interstate; it's against the law."

We also find ourselves facing another inexplicable fact that doesn't seem to follow logically: if bigger is better, then why the existence of so many small churches? They're everywhere, with something like 75 percent of America's churches having less than 90 people at worship on Sunday morning and 50 percent less than 35 at worship.

One denominational official said of small churches, "You can't grow 'em and you can't kill 'em!" Another joked, "God sure must have loved small churches, because he made so many of them!"

If we resonate to "Life doesn't happen along the interstates," maybe we'll also resonate to David Ray's book title and faith statement: *Small Churches Are the Right Size.*[2] Ray asserts that small churches are just the right size for being faithful and effective churches. That's not to say large churches are the wrong size, for they obviously fulfill needs and provide much ministry, too. It's simply an experience-based belief that small churches ought not to be demeaned or diminished, that they have much to offer in their witness and faithfulness.

Small churches are the right size. That resonates in me. Maybe sometimes our guts are smarter than either our heads or the society's wisdom, and we ought to listen. Small churches are indeed the right size.

Douglas Walrath, a former judicatory official with the Reformed Church in America and retired Director of Bangor Seminary's Small-Church Leadership Program, writes, "probably defining the small church is a function of purpose [not size], and no single definition serves all purposes. In a world of rising institutional costs, small means marginal, unable to make it institutionally in one or more respects. [But] small also means a certain quality of life, a group where people know about one another and where relationships matter more than people."[3]

Not long ago I was at a deacons' meeting of the small church I pastored in Vermont. We met in someone's home, not in the church. We had almost no business on our agenda—three or four short items besides the secretary's and treasurer's reports. And yet we weren't there just for business. We shared concerns about a number of people in our church and in our community. We asked about one another's families and jobs and homes and security. We dared to venture into personal areas of one another's lives rather than just stick with the task of a business meeting. We cared about one another. We spoke of local people facing cancer and cancer treatments. We imagined the impact a young mother's death would have on our community and on her family. One or two of us were near tears, and we could all feel the emotional tension we were sharing. Although we weren't attending to much formal business, we were attending to the business of life.

Bill Diehl, a Lutheran layperson and author, argues that size does indeed make a big difference when it comes to authentic Christian community. He says: "Most congregations need to have several hundred members in order to be viable. How does one relate in an experiential way to a hundred other persons? The brief encounters we have with others as we come and go from Sunday worship services hardly lend themselves to sharing one's faith experiences. And when the congregation does break the larger group into smaller units it is usually for a specific task. The church council meets not in order to support the faith of each other, but to do the work of running the organization. Same with all the committees of the congregation. They meet to do their assigned tasks, not to be a place where people share questions about how one relates faith to daily life. Sometimes the choir can become a small Christian community, but usually it is by accident rather than by intent."[4]

Maybe it's been by accident—I suppose it is—but our small church's deacons frequently experienced that "small Christian community" Bill Diehl refers to. I'm sure many small-church boards and committees do, too.

One young student pastor I supervised had a very difficult time understanding the small church meetings at his church. He wanted to accomplish the business (the tasks), but the group always spent the first half-hour "checking in" and asking questions like "How're the kids? And how's your mother adjusting to the nursing home?" Then, at the end of the meeting, they'd all stand around for another 15 or 20 minutes while they asked more of those chit-chatty types of questions. Sandwiched into the 45 minutes between socializing was what he thought was the business, but the important stuff—the business of life—was more likely conducted in the before-and-after time slot!

We need to recognize smallness not as a deficit or a deficiency, but as a virtue. No matter what society's values, no matter what television or business or even our denominational statisticians and planners preach, we need realize that our guts are resonating when we hear the statement, "Small churches are the right size."

When I spoke recently with a group of Episcopal priests from Virginia small churches we found it quite surprising that, in ranking 11 tasks or functions associated with the church and/or the pastoral office, evangelism came out quite low, and many of them felt resentful about the expectation that was being forced upon them. Their rating evangelism so low felt like it was bordering on the heretical—considering the fact that their diocesan bishop had just declared (in big, bold letters) the '90s to be "The Decade of Evangelism!" But I heard and felt what they were saying, and I had heard and felt many other small-church pastors say the same. These pastors were saying the small church is already a wonderful-sized community in which to make disciples. And isn't that our commission—to make disciples (which is different than making members or church supporters)? Because it is an ideal size for making disciples, you don't need to add to the small church significantly for it to be OK. What those Virginia pastors wanted to do was to work on depth of faith rather than focus all their energies on signing up new members or gaining new converts. They perceived—correctly, I believe—that the task today is different than it was in the earliest days of a fledging New Testament church which was trying desperately to establish itself. Back then the task might well have been signing up members and forming Christian churches. Now we're faced with a country where people are almost born Christians, but they are "nominal Christians," immature in their faith. So it's the job of the community—especially of the small-church community—to nurture these fledglings, to disciple them, and equip them for service, not to the church, but to the world.

In "Conversion within the Church," Quaker theologian Elton Trueblood argues that the greatest field for Christian evangelism today is in the church. "The task before us is clear," he writes. "The task is to try to reach the present membership of churches with a message of such vitality that they experience a conversion within the church, rather than a conversion to the church."[5]

Trueblood makes sense. We've been so focused on signing people up, so caught up in reversing numerical declines, that we stand in danger of neglecting people's spiritual needs. In some cases we've gotten them in the doors on a promise, but we haven't delivered—because we're still facing the outside, spouting promises. Meanwhile, our fears and the pressures that threaten institutional survival force us to campaigns, drives, buzzwords, and bumper stickers. But the calls for evangelism and church growth are made for the wrong reasons. The rallying cry isn't raised in order to have us convert people or to make disciples; it's to float the institutions and to keep the denominations healthy.

Even worse, we have bought into the world's message that we've got to be "successful." Instead of falling prey to that subliminal temptation, we need to remember: Jesus didn't call us to be successful, and Jesus didn't call us to grow; Jesus called us to be faithful, to make disciples.

Presbyterian small-church specialist James Cushman hits the nail on the head when he writes that "almost all small churches are unsuccessful. In success-oriented American society, small churches do not measure up to any of the standards of success. They don't grow fast. They don't have much money. Most of the important people don't attend small churches. They usually don't have exciting and innovative programs of ministry to the community. They are not on the cutting edge of theology. By every measurable standard, small churches are unsuccessful."[6] By those standards, almost all of the small churches I've ever served or consulted with have been "unsuccessful." In my last parish we weren't growing fast; we didn't have much money; most of the "important" people didn't attend our church (though the people who attended were important). Our programs were quite good, but I doubt many people would describe our small church as having "exciting and innovative programs of ministry to the community." We probably weren't on the cutting edge of theology. So, by those standards, our small church was not successful.

But in God's eyes, in embracing the call to struggle with our faith, in our efforts to love one another as God has loved us, in our efforts to seek justice and to feed the hungry and clothe the naked, in our attempts to make disciples—in all these things we sought to respond faithfully to God's calling. Even if we failed in the world's eyes and flopped by the world's standards—if we remained faithful and tried our best to be a nurturing Christian community, we were successful.

When I got ready to leave my small home church to attend seminary, my wife and I were invited to join the minister at the altar rail on our last Sunday there. The minister said something to the congregation about us responding to a calling, and he said the congregation's blessing ought to accompany us. As we knelt there he laid hands on our heads and prayed a farewell blessing on the church's behalf.

It was powerful and nurturing. Yet it didn't make a mark on the world's yardstick for success any more than the deacon's meeting I mentioned earlier. Nor was "success" registered on the world's yardstick the Sunday a trembling 11-year-old boy made his solo singing debut in a small church in Bethel, Vermont. He sang as his father's fingers strummed the guitar and his stepmother's eyes filled with tears. Isn't it sad that none of those events—by the standards for success in today's world—would be deemed "successful?"

But maybe small churches aren't supposed to be successful. Maybe, just maybe, David Ray is right and small churches are the right size—for worship, for service, for making disciples. I believe there is a special place in God's heart for the small church (for God made so many of them!).

After all, God does seem to care especially for the marginalized and the disadvantaged, the poor, the weak, the outcasts—those society marks as "unsuccessful." But didn't God choose "what is foolish in the world to shame the wise, what is weak in the world to shame the strong, what is low and despised in the world, even things that are not, to bring to nothing things that are?" (1 Corinthians 1:27-28). Maybe we need to remember that the very "stone the builders rejected [as unsuitable] has become the cornerstone" (Mark 12:10-11). That's what the small church is or can be—the cornerstone for true, faithful, life-giving Christian community.

Instead of insisting that each small church grow into a different entity—in the process changing its nature and perhaps losing its strongest discipline elements, in the process selling its soul—maybe our denominational growth ought to come from forming more small churches, more single-celled caring groups, more intimate way-stations for "equipping the saints for ministry" (Ephesians 4:1 2).

Bill Diehl writes, "It is necessary, I am convinced, for God's faithful people also to be a part of a smaller community of Christians which can add a different dimension to their faith lives. The small Christian support group can supply that which the larger congregation cannot."[7]

We've got a tremendous resource in this institution the world seems to mock, in this stone the builders reject, in this Body of Christ we call the small church. God chose what is weak to shame the strong, what is foolish to shame to wise, and declared the stone the builders rejected would become the cornerstone. Let's thank God for our small churches today, and let's esteem them and learn from them, for when it comes to doing the work of God—small churches are the right size.

NOTES

1. William Least Heat Moon, *Blue Highways: A Journey into America* (New York: Fawcett Crest, 1982), p. 10.

2. David R. Ray, *Small Churches Are the Right Size* (New York: Pilgrim Press, 1982), p. xiv.

3. Douglas Walrath in *New Possibilities for Small Churches*, ed. Douglas Alan Walrath (New York: Pilgrim Press, 1983), p. xi.

4. William E. Diehl, *In Search of Faithfulness: Lessons from the Christian Community* (Philadelphia: Fortress, 1987), p. 67.

5. Quoted in Diehl, *Faithfulness*, pp. 66-67.

6. James Cushman, *Beyond Survival* (Ropley, Va.: James Cushman, 1981), p. 1.
7. Diehl, Faithfulness, p. 69.

Originally published in The Five Stones *(Summer 1996), pp. 2-6; used by permission.*

Part Three
BUILDING THE CAPACITY
OF THE
SMALL CHURCH

Chapter 15

BUILDING UP, BREAKING UP, GETTING UP

Anthony G. Pappas

Some churches program welcoming. They select their extroverted members and visit them upon their visitors (after due training, of course). But small churches must do welcoming as part of their nature, their very way of being. Pastors and leaders can encourage this capacity in their small church. Here's how.

A strong, healthy small church feels wonderful from the inside. You know people. You know what people's strengths are. You receive life and joy and strength and encouragement from who they are. You know the particular gifts that God has given them. This world isn't full of surprises. You know what's going to happen. You know who sits in this pew and you know who's the first one in and the first one out of church. And there's good fellowship. You know when you have a hurt there's going to be people there for you. You are not alone. You are connected. Inside a healthy small church is a beautiful place.

But that's the problem. Somebody described the small church as a loaf of French bread. If you can break it open, the taste and the aroma and the texture and the nutrition are wonderful—but just try to break it open! There is this big hard crust on the outside. How do you get through that? I think that the only way to break open that crust is to realize that we're dealing with a social fabric. Evangelism in the small church is the living out and the sharing of the Good News of Jesus Christ. Good news—embodied in a healthy social fabric. The small church, though, tends by its own nature to fold in on itself and build a hard crust. How do we open up the small church for evangelism? How can we make the small church more welcoming? We can open up the small church through building up (attitude), breaking up (relationships), and getting up (behavior).

BUILDING UP

"Building up" has to do with the attitude of small-church people. We want to build up their self-esteem. Many small churches have an attitude of defensiveness, and this comes about through multiple rejections. They do not want to promote their church to others because that hasn't worked in the past. People have often rejected it. How do we build up the congregation's self-esteem so that rejection does not stop the enterprise of invitation?

1. The first means to help correct this is through *language, speaking*. Pastors can *start talking a language of health*, building a world of words that then helps to shape how people view the rest of life. We can talk about the fact that the people of God can be a positive force as God intended them to be. We can talk about the truths that size is not a success criterion of a Christian. Let's talk rather about faithfulness or service as success criteria and not size per se. Another thing we can talk about is that Christ's body has inherent integrity. Where two or more are gathered in Christ's name, there is the presence of God. Isn't that what the Bible tells us? Therein is your church's integrity. Two or more can worship, can pray together, share together, support one another. They can be learning and growing; they can do something in the community wherever they may be. In China, by law, they couldn't do anything evangelistically, but just getting together and being loyal and not betraying others was a testimony to the community. Just being faithful was service to the community. That is what the church can be. Small is beautiful. Lift it up. Share it. Love it.

2. The second means is to *reinforce the good*. Do you remember the proverbial glass—half-full or half-empty? It's very important which half you look at. Many of us who are trained for success by objective criteria, by numeric criteria, look at the empty half. We're not doing this. Only two people showed up for that. We only have three kids in our youth group. That's what it means to look at the empty half. So what if three kids show up? Do something with them—have a good time; encourage their growth and their life. If your people do something positive, encourage it.

3. The third means is to *do things that bring about successes*. Take things in bite-size chunks. Don't say, "We're going to evangelize everyone in a three-county area." Rather, say, "Let's go to everybody within a block of the church. Let's visit them and let them know we exist." Whatever is appropriate in your situation, set a goal that your people can do and feel good about doing. Build up the sense of "Hey, we can't do everything but

we sure can do a few things pretty darn good." Then they have the confidence to tackle something else. Build up self-esteem.

BREAKING UP

Once attitudes are built up, it's time to break up. Break up the monolithic structure. The problem in a small church is that a newcomer can't find a place to nest, to grab on, to sit down, to be a part of things—so swish, they just slide right on by and right on out. There are three things we can do about this.

1. One is to *rewrite the story*. I found out a few years ago that I have a second cousin that I never knew about. My grandmother and my cousin's grandmother had argued 100 years ago, and even though we grew up and lived in towns that are only a few miles away from each other, we never even knew of each other's existence. But, out of the blue, she showed up at a family funeral. After two generations, we didn't know we were supposed to be angry with each other, so we became friends instead. What a live wire! She's short, wider than she is tall, and full of life and energy—she's a joy to have in the family. Well, now I have to rewrite the story of my relatives to include her. She was always there, but I didn't know it. The story of my family excluded her. The stories of congregations exclude people, either through ignorance or deliberately. We need to rewrite the story and say, "There are a whole lot of lost relatives out there. Let's welcome them in. They may not be biologically connected, but they'll be spiritually connected if they meet in the name of Jesus Christ." Remember the strangers that Abraham fed? Remember the angels that we're supposed to entertain unaware? We can rewrite that story of who is in our family if we want to.

2. A second way to break open relationships is to *encourage bridge people*. Bridge people are the people that stand at the bridges from the congregation to the community. They let people cross the bridge over the moat so they can get into the castle or they keep them out. These are the people who are in the church but also have significant connections to people outside the church. These are the people you want to encourage. Encourage their welcoming, their openness, their warmth; help them to let people in.

3. A third way to break open the small church's social structure is to *nurture the rebel within*. Suppose I came to your small church tomorrow

and said, "Look, here's what we're going to do. We're going to be an evangelizing community and you do this, this, and this." There wouldn't be much surprise what would happen to me. I'd be on the next train out of town. You have to be part of the small church before you're going to be allowed to have a significant enough place to change it. But one who is totally socialized into the congregation's culture will not want to change it. Instead, look to the family rebel. Sometimes that rebellion is good. When the church is not in a healthy and open enough position, rebellion against the status quo in order to be more faithful is a very good thing. Find out who in your congregation has a greater vision for faithfulness than the congregation as a whole has. Nurture that person. Encourage that person. Give him or her space to affect the vision.

GETTING UP

Build up the attitude of your small church. Break up the monolithic social structure. And then get up and go. The first problem we addressed is attitude, the second problem is social structure, the third problem is that the range of our behaviors isn't wide enough to let people in. How can we broaden the range of congregational activities?

1. First, we need to engage in *high-service, low-threat activities*. In my community this means covered-dish suppers and fairs on the front lawn. People come and they find out something about the church and find out who's in the church. There's no threat to them. They don't have to be converted to come to these events. This is how we establish contact with people. So do bonding, not exclusionary, activities.

2. Second, try to *exclude those exclusionary activities*. The story is told of a new family who came to a supper at the church. They brought a pie and a can of whipped topping and covered the pie with the nondairy topping. The women in the church were horrified. Their families were dairy farmers, so they took the pie and threw it in the trashcan. Now, you tell me: Do you think that family ever came back to that church? Find out what things keep people away and try to replace them with open, welcoming activities.

3. Finally, remember to *preserve continuity in change*. The small church is oriented to the past. It doesn't like to change. The good leader in a small church who wants to open it up will introduce changes in ways that

can be handled. First is to realize that evolution is better than revolution: maintain a slow and steady timeframe. Tinker with this and then tinker with that. Don't butcher any sacred cows. There are things that are symbolic, that have meaning out of proportion. Sometimes you have to do things in a parallel manner. The old group wants this and the new group wants that. That's fine. They're both valid. No problem. Parallel activities give people different places to buy in. And don't wear everybody out. Have fun in all this. Throw a party. Have a picnic. Take things step by step. Be happy. Live in Christ's joy. No one's going to come to a church that isn't happy and healthy. If you've got the Good News of Jesus Christ, then you'll be much more apt to receive positive responses to your invitation.

CONCLUSION

I'm really thrilled about small churches. I think they show us how God planned human beings to live from the beginning of time. I think that's what heaven is going to be like, so I'm looking forward to heaven, too! But I don't feel that unfaithfulness or falling short of our God-given nature is part of what being a small church is all about. I think the small church can be a beautifully warm and inviting and open place. We can be all of that and if we are, others will feel welcome and find God's healing touch in our fellowship.

Originally published in The Five Stones *(Fall 1994), pp. 2, 20-21; used by permission.*

Chapter 16

BUILDING ON THE CAPACITIES
OF
SMALL-MEMBERSHIP CHURCHES

Clay Smith

The work of community-development researcher John McKnight—
especially his ideas about capacity-building models versus deficiency
models of people and communities—has been helpful for those working to
rebuild rural and urban communities from the inside out. McKnight encourages us to focus on the capacities (people, groups, associations, and so
forth) that are present and work for renewal based on these capacities. A
deficiency model, by contrast, focuses on what is not present and designs
delivery service systems to fill the gaps. McKnight believes that real community happens when folks share their capacities. Deficiency models, on
the other hand, create clients and dependent relationships and undermine
real community.

These concepts can be very helpful for those of us who work with
small-membership congregations. We often struggle with a denominational
system (and with value systems within our culture) that looks at the small-
membership church and sees only its deficiencies. We know them well:
"We don't have enough—people, children, youth, young adults, young families, program, money, facilities, vision, Sunday School teachers, commitment, and so forth." The list can go on and on. The small-membership
church thus becomes more defined by what it lacks.

Part of our task as leaders with small-membership churches is to move
beyond the stereotypes of deficiency to claim the capacities for ministry
that we find over and over again within these congregations. The staff at
Hinton Rural Life Center works individually with about 40 such congregations every year. What we find is this:

• Small-membership churches have many gifted and committed leaders
  who have a deep desire for their church to do well.

- About 40 percent of the people in rural communities are unchurched—a great opportunity for service and growth.
- Small-membership churches are located in almost every community—strategically located for mission and ministry. Many persons in our society prefer a small-membership, family-style church experience where they will be known by name.
- Most small-membership churches can grow in commitment, spiritual depth, program, giving, outreach, and numbers.

Small-membership churches are about relational ministry. We are like extended families. We can be known, we can accept and affirm others, we can be intergenerational. We can love people one person at a time. We can be family to those in our community who have no family.

Small-membership churches have a strong sense of history and shared experience. We have lots of stories to share. When the outsiders hear our story, and when we take time to hear their story, then the extended family can grow to include new people.

Small-membership churches know about the importance of place—a place to believe and to belong. Whenever I enter the chancel area of a small-membership church I often wonder about the sacred encounters that have occurred there: the professions of faith, baptisms, weddings, funerals. We even know what it means to have a special place to sit within this sacred space. Many persons in our communities, especially those who are unchurched, have no place in small-membership churches. We can learn to share our space and create a place for those who have none.

Small-membership churches often have influence and presence in their communities that is out of all proportion to their small size. Just look around when you attend the next civic group, PTA, school-board meeting, or community-planning group and count the number of church members. Small-membership churches possess great capacity, through our members, to work for good across the whole community.

Labeling the small-membership church as deficient diminishes its ability to be resourceful and responsive as members work together to build a healthier congregation and reach out to the surrounding community. Focusing on the capacities that are already there opens up many new possibilities for building a healthy, Christ-centered community of faith.

Originally published in The Five Stones *(Summer 2000), p. 15; used by permission.*

Chapter 17

COOKING ON A LIMITED BUDGET: MAXIMIZING THE SMALLER CHURCH'S MINISTRY POTENTIAL

John M. Koessler

The wife of one of our church's leaders came to me with a complaint: "Several of the older members feel that you aren't meeting their needs." "What should I be doing differently?" I asked. She thought for a moment, then to my frustration replied, "I don't know. But they feel like the church has forgotten them."

Although I didn't have a solution, I could understand the criticism. The young singles had expressed similar feelings. In a way they were both correct. Our congregation is primarily made up of families with young children. As a result, while our Christian education ministries are very strong, there is currently very little for either singles or seniors.

Others have expressed frustration with the adult Sunday school program. They wonder why our church can't offer a large selection of electives every quarter. The parents of teenagers would like a large youth program with weekly planned activities for their children.

The problem of limited resources is one of the greatest discouragements of small-church ministry. It always seems that there is too much to be done and too little to do it with. While it is still possible for a small church like ours to really "cook," we must learn to do so on a limited budget.

The availability of human resources is a function of our size. While the opportunities for ministry before us are limitless, our capacity to be effective is not. Consequently, a realistic evaluation of the gifts and opportunities God has placed before the church has forced us to specialize. As a result, our church has gained the reputation of being a "kid-friendly" church. Over the years we have developed several very effective children's ministries.

Because we realize that it is impossible for us to be all things to all people, we are concentrating our efforts in the specific areas where God has especially equipped us. Research analyst George Barna has noted that this same approach has been a key factor in the success of many larger churches. Barna observes that an organization is most successful when it strives for excellence in its own area of expertise. While smaller churches may be more sensitive to their limitations, the fact is that every church, regardless of its size, struggles with this problem. In his book *User-Friendly Churches*, Barna points out, "the stark reality is that every church has limited resources, and has been called to accomplish a specific mission."[1]

In his study of successful churches, Barna found that those who were most effective deliberately limited their ministry, allowing their focus to be shaped by the availability of resources and their ability to achieve excellence in targeted areas. The smaller church is exceptionally positioned to practice this principle.

An awareness that God has not called us to be all things to all people can have a liberating effect on the church's mission. It means that we can stop trying to fill round holes with square pegs. Instead of setting programs in place first and then staffing them with the reluctant, the disinterested, or the ill suited, we can begin by designing programs around people's interests and abilities.

Approaching the task of programming with this perspective helps the church's leaders to be more sensitive to what might be called "gift clusters" in the congregation. A gift cluster is a grouping of spiritual gifts or individual interests. These groupings are usually found in the church's strongest ministries.

For example, although we live in a farming community, we have an unusually high number of educators in our congregation. Consequently, our field of specialization has been in the area of Christian education. In another church the gifts and interests might cluster around the areas of music and worship, while others might find that their programs are weighted in the area of teen ministries or community service.

The small church will increase its impact even more when its field of specialization fills a gap or addresses a felt need in the community. If the other churches in our town already had an effective children's program in place, we would not have experienced the same measure of success.

By identifying the gift clusters in the congregation, the small church can approach its ministry with the assumption that God has equipped it to serve the community in a unique way. Instead of being seen as a liability, the church's size becomes one of the factors that contributes to its overall effectiveness.

Like the young girl who measures herself by the false standard of today's "supermodels," small churches who try to be something God has not called them to be plan for failure and the inevitable feelings of inferiority that result. Fred Smith observes, "As I've visited small churches, in none of the healthy ones are there any apologies for size or scope of program. They recognize they are a different organization altogether. While both they and the megachurch are under the Lordship of Christ, their functions and ways of performing are different."[2]

Specialization gives the small church the freedom to aspire to excellence rather than *omnicompetence*, but it also has the potential to breed an unhealthy spirit of perfectionism. Although we would like our ministries to be professional, the blunt reality is that most of them are performed by amateurs. The church that decides that all its musicians must possess the singing ability of a recording star before they are allowed to perform will soon find that it has no music ministry.

Our board was reviewing a list of potential elders when one of the men complained, "I am not sure any of these are really qualified." He did not mean to be overly critical. But his level of expectation was so high that no one in the congregation could have possibly measured up to it. I pointed out that the longer he served on the board the higher his standard would become, since he was using himself as a reference point. In reality, most of the people we were considering were at about the same level of spiritual maturity as he had been when he first came on the board.

We need to balance our quest for excellence with a determination to create an environment where God's people can explore new areas of giftedness. In other words, we must provide ample opportunities for them to learn new skills in an atmosphere that allows freedom to develop and to fail. It is unfair to expect someone who is at the beginning of their ministry experience to possess the same level of expertise as one who has been serving in the same capacity for 10 or 20 years. Our choices must be based on an appreciation for the potential someone has for future ministry rather than focusing solely on their current ability to perform.

Realistically evaluating our church's ministry potential also means that we must come to grips with the fact that there are some areas where God has called us to mediocrity. There are times when a job poorly done is better than no job at all. For years I was frustrated by the performance of our church choir. In my opinion, they did not practice enough. Instead of selecting their music on the basis of its potential for enhancing worship, they picked pieces that were easy to sing. It seemed to me that they sang the same numbers over and over again. Secretly, I wished that the old choir would dissolve so that we could replace it with a more quality program.

Eventually I got my wish. Unfortunately, instead of seeing a new choir dedicated to excellence in performance rise in its place. I watched as our church's entire music ministry went into a state of decline. Now I wish we had the old choir, with all its imperfections, back in place. The spirit of perfectionism is really not an element in the quest for excellence but a dysfunctional compulsion that will crush the spirit of our churches.

While realism is indispensable when charting the course of the smaller church, it is essential that we couple realism with creativity. Otherwise our honest assessment of the limited resources at our disposal will probably lead to discouragement. What is creativity and how do we develop it? To some it is a nebulous quality which the gifted few possess and the rest do not. This view of the creative process is epitomized in the comment made by painter Salvador Dali to one of his admirers. "Is it hard to paint a picture?" she asked. "No," Dali replied, "it is either easy or it is impossible."

According to this view, one is either creative or one is not. To those who possess the skill, creative thinking comes effortlessly. The rest may as well give up. However, while it may be true that creative thinking comes more easily to some than to others, I believe that with a little effort everyone can be creative to some degree. All it takes is a paradigm shift.

Stephen R. Covey refers to this shift in his book *The Seven Habits of Highly Effective People* and notes that the term was introduced by Thomas Kuhn in *The Structures of Scientific Revolutions*. Covey explains: "Kuhn shows how almost every significant breakthrough in the field of scientific endeavor is first a break with tradition, with old ways of thinking, with old paradigms."[3]

Covey goes on to explain that a good example of this concept in action can be found in the Copernican revolution. Prior to Copernicus it was generally accepted that the earth was the center of the solar system. When Copernicus placed the Sun at the center of his model, he not only changed the shape of science but also man's perception of the entire universe.

How do we shift gears and begin thinking creatively? We can start by thinking positively. The tendency of the smaller church is to concentrate on what it is unable to do. When we attempt to think in visionary terms we constantly fight against the mentality that says,"We're only a small church. There is only so much we can do."

It is true that we must be realistic if we want our goals to be achievable. But it is just as important that we have a sense of divine calling. Realism without a sense of calling will lead to a defeatist mentality. Our perspective of the church's ministry will change radically when we recognize that instead of being expected to do the impossible, we have been called to accomplish the mission for which God has also uniquely equipped us.

Another important aspect of creative thinking is the determination to use what we have. Copernicus changed the paradigm but not the facts. He worked with the same basic data used by his predecessors. Too often I waste my time trying to change the data:

If we only had more people. . . .
If only we had more money. . . .
If only our people were musically inclined. . . .
If only we had more singles. . . .

God has not called me to minister with what I do not have but with the resources placed at my disposal. It is not the data that needs to be changed but my perception of it.

Being willing to borrow is another key to creative ministry. While originality may be an essential aspect of creativity in the arts, it is not nearly as important in ministry. Adaptability is far more crucial to our success than originality. When I evaluate a new project the critical question is not, "Has anyone done this before?" but rather, "Will it work here?"

Every evening throughout the summer a crowd of teens gathers on the corner across from the high school parking lot. For months I watched them and wished we could find some way to impact them for Christ. I decided to try thinking like a missionary. "If this were a small village in a foreign country," I asked myself, "and I were a missionary, what would I do?"

I had been impressed with the phenomenal success that many mission organizations were reporting with the film *Jesus*. Their method was simple and cost effective. Find an accessible spot, draw a crowd, and show the film. Borrowing from this already proven strategy, we made plans to host "Movies on Main Street." We set up a projector and showed teen-oriented evangelistic films on the door of a utility shed in the high school parking lot for three consecutive Saturday nights in August. During the films we gave away free popcorn and soda and passed out gospel tracts. Every evening we ministered to from 40 to 50 people. Was it creative? I think so. But it wasn't original.

Ideas aren't the only things that we can draw on for creative ministry. Resources can be borrowed as well. This is accomplished through networking. One group of churches has joined together with a Christian camp to provide a ministry for its teens. Individually, none of these churches is able to afford a youth director. But in return for minimal financial support, they are able to use the camp's full-time staff worker as a kind of adjunct youth director. He organizes a Wednesday night Bible study and activity which is attended by the combined youth of the churches and rotates its location from week to week.

Perhaps the most important ingredient in the creative process is the freedom to fail. Creative people are willing to take risks. The potential for return outweighs their fear of failure. According to the stereotype, the pastor is a person of vision who is constantly being checked by the church board. The pastor sees far into the future and dreams of what the church might become. Board members, on the other hand, are bound by the limitations of the present and are desperately trying to hold on to what the church has already accomplished.

In reality, I find that I am the one who is more likely to discourage visionary thinking. When someone proposes a new ministry, I am liable to be the first to raise an objection. I constantly battle against my tendency to be overly cautious. Why am I so negative, when I really do want the church to be on the cutting edge? The answer is simple. I am afraid of failure. Although I know that it is wrong, I identify my personal success with that of the church.

However, anyone who has experienced true success will be the first to tell you that success is often preceded by failure. Thomas Edison performed 50,000 experiments before he discovered the right elements that enabled him to develop a new storage battery. When he was finished someone asked him if he was frustrated that so little had resulted from so much work. "Results?" the inventor replied. "Why, I have gotten a lot of results. I know 50,000 things that won't work."

The most successful salesman is also the one who has lost more sales than any of his peers. The ball player who hit the most home runs last season probably struck out more times than the rest of his teammates. The pastor who experiences the most success is the one who isn't afraid of failure.

Finally, realism and creativity must be combined with faith. Without faith realism will choke out creativity and degenerate into pessimism. J. Oswald Sanders identifies visionary faith as one of the essential qualities of leadership: "Those who have most powerfully and permanently influenced their generation have been the 'seers'—men who have seen more and farther than others—men of faith, for faith is vision."[4] In other words, realism must be balanced with "the Gideon factor." Imagine how incredible it must have sounded to Gideon when God told him that he had too many men to defeat the Midianites (Judges 7:2). Those who take the Gideon factor into account recognize that God often prefers to use small numbers when accomplishing great things.

On a gloomy Monday morning, after I had grumbled to the Lord about our church's size for the thousandth time, Gideon's victory came to mind and a disturbing thought occurred to me. Wasn't it true that my desire to see the church grow in numbers was partially a reflection of my sinful tendency to depend upon the arm of flesh instead of the Lord? Was it possible that God had deliberately kept our church's numbers small, in order to demonstrate that our successes came from God and not as a result of human effort?

Viewed from this perspective every church, regardless of size, can draw from infinite resources. The attendance figures and size of our budget are irrevelant. We all have access to the same unlimited resources: "Such confidence is ours through Christ before God. Not that we are competent to claim anything for ourselves, but our competence comes from God" (2 Cor. 3:4-5).

The seniors are still grumbling. The singles still want a group of their own. I don't have a solution. Not yet. But I do have the confidence that God has provided us with all that we need to get the job done.

NOTES

1. George Barna, *User-Friendly Churches* (Ventura, Calif.: Regal Books, 1991), p. 51.
2. Fred Smith, "The Unique Role of the Small Church," *Leadership* (Fall 1991), p. 87.
3. Stephen R. Covey, *The Seven Habits of Highly Effective* People (New York: Simon & Schuster, 1989), p. 29.
4. J. Oswald Sanders, *Spiritual Leadership* (Chicago: Moody Press, 1986), p. 71.

Originally published in The Five Stones *(Summer 1994), pp. 20-23; used by permission.*

Chapter 18
GAINING THE RURAL ADVANTAGE
Kenneth R.. Marple

In 1965, my wife, Gloria, and I left the mountains of north central Pennsylvania to pastor our first church in a small rural village in Washington state. In the 28 years since that time, the world has changed more than we could have guessed. Today, the world is on the run 365 days a year, seven days a week, 24 hours a day. What does this mean to a minister? It means that many of your people will work a Sunday shift every other week. Vacations, family visits and reunions, outings, emergencies, sickness, and bad weather will make a sizable dent in the remaining Sundays. Let me translate this into reality for your Sunday worship service: it means that your church must have approximately 250 very faithful, active worshipers to generate 100 worshipers on a given Sunday morning! It also means that the face of the congregation will be quite different from Sunday to Sunday. It could mean that specific worshipers will only cross paths with each other one Sunday in eight.

At that first little Baptist church, on the bank of the Columbia River, it only took about 100 active worshipers to generate an attendance of 75. In our present church, in the Endless Mountains of the Northeast, a nearby factory begins its seven-day-a-week seasonal schedule in mid-July, then abruptly lays off in November. After layoff, it could be several more Sundays before I get to see these hard-working parishioners, since their personal privation is usually at the breaking point and they need to take some well-deserved trips!

As ministers, it's important to realize that we and our congregations are caught *together* in these powerful changes. I prefer to deal with it by being thankful each time a parishioner attends, rather than complaining about the times he or she isn't there. In addition, as a minister, I am fully aware that it will take at least twice the number of congregants to generate the same size worship service of three decades ago. If such issues are not clearly understood, the result is likely to be feelings of false guilt on the part of the minister, congregation, or both.

Beyond these general changes, rural churches have their own specific economic, demographic, community, urban influence, and threshold of ministry issues to deal with. Each issue has a negative as well as a positive. Good rural ministry is accomplished by accenting the positive and downplaying the negative.

RURAL ECONOMICS

Negative Considerations. Per-household incomes are considerably lower in rural areas. Certainly this will impact on the operating budget of the church, the minister's salary and retirement, as well as the type of ministry options available to the rural church. However, there is an additional spin-off of low household income: In order to *stay functionally* within the middle class, rural people do everything for themselves! They remodel or even build their own houses, do their own upkeep, chop their own wood (literally), maintain their own automobiles, grow and process their own fruits and vegetables, and raise or hunt for (then process) their own meat. If that were not enough, many rural folk also have an additional cottage-type mini-business. They do woodworking, sew, or otherwise "moonlight" their skills to neighbors and friends. All of this has a definite negative impact on time and labor available for church ministries and activities.

Positive Perspectives. By nature, rural folk are hardworking. This means that they will generally "squeeze out" time for anything they consider necessary. If they share a vision of Christ's love in any given church ministry, they will support it with labor. They may be late, but they will be there! The "do-it-yourself" mentality of rural people can translate into lower church expenses as rural congregations combine their various skills at church work days. Both of our two congregations completed major construction projects with volunteer labor. The "hands-on" physical labor actually produces a valuable sense of ownership. Urban churches seldom have this advantage. The spirit of Christ's love has found an outlet numerous times as our congregation rallied together for a barn raising, or to lay cement block basements for fire victims. Rural folk have their shining times!

Rural Demographics

Negative Considerations. The area in which I serve has a population density of 25 people per square mile within its school district. The population of the entire township is 1,119. Most of the young people who grew up within this rural congregation will end up moving to urban areas. Many retiring folk move to Florida, taking their experience, wisdom, and capital with them. Those who do not move south will often own a winter home in the south.

In addition to these obvious demographic handicaps, the rural church will eventually pass on some of its resources to the town church as a direct result of community infrastructure. Schools are generally located in the large service towns as are a concentration of apartments for rent, senior housing units, and health-care facilities. An additional loss to the rural congregation will gradually occur as older people retire into senior housing units located in such towns. Since schools are generally in town, school release-time programs will be held in the town church, thereby increasing the exposure of even rural children to the higher population situation.

Ministries that are possible where people are concentrated are not as supportable when Mom has to drive 15 miles to drop Danny off at youth fellowship, then another 15 miles to pick him up. Though some rural churches have tried to make up for the disadvantage with buses, there are strong negatives here. For example, population sparseness demands great amounts of time on the road, while many miles must be covered. There is also the ethical issue of taking a bus to another small rural town to pick up people where a neighbor church is struggling with the same situation. Perhaps the disgruntled people who might be prone to ride the bus to your church would be better reconciled to the church in the neighboring towns. Let's face it: It is different when you're not in the service town.

Positive Perspectives and Solutions. I have a friend in Elmira, New York, who owns several stores. Early in my ministry here, I asked him to speak at the annual "home gathering" of our rural church. After the service, he told me a story: "I have two shoe stores; one is in the old downtown section, the other is at the mall. The people-traffic at the mall is so great that I only have to sell to a small percentage of the people who walk by. However, at my downtown store I must do something to actually *attract* the people. I have to do things to make it their destination. As I drove in to speak at your church today, I noticed that you're not in the mall traffic, so you'd better make yourself into *a destination*."

That advice is central to rural ministry solutions. The rural church must not be afraid to advertise its presence. The minister needs to make sure the church has a reasonably high profile. He or she must serve on various community boards and organizations. A column in the local paper could certainly help. Our church just adopted the highway coming into our little town. In return, the state of Pennsylvania has erected signs announcing, "The next two miles of highway adopted by the Austinville Union Church." Take full advantage of the free community event calendars available in many newspapers, pennysavers, and radio stations.

In many ways, the rural church must work harder. Since it is increasingly difficult to start things that people must commit to for "every Tuesday night for the rest of their lives," you might try specific, one-shot workshops that appeal to a variety of interests within the community. For example, form a resource pool with five or six other ministers in your region. Each minister then prepares a workshop on just one given subject. Though you will have to present your workshop at five other churches, you'll only have to prepare one, while your church will get the benefit of six! Pull qualified lay people into the project.

Because we work with greater distances, we try to group extra activities into one day here at Austinville. On Wednesdays, a ladies' Bible study meets at 2 P.M., a children's club at 4 P.M., prayer meetings at 7 P.M., choir at 8 P.M., and cantata practice at 8:30 P.M.! This not only cuts down on travel, but keeps from breaking up the family as a result of dominating numerous evenings. In addition, the conservation of gas is ecologically sound.

COMMUNITY

Negative Considerations. Because of the interrelated nature of rural communities, small offenses can have a heavy impact on a rural church. For example, if Aunt Sally has a tiff with cousin Fred, it could result in a family fight that keeps three or four families out of church. Or if Brewbaker's cows get out and eat Putman's garden, two families may be absent from church on Sunday morning. The rural grapevine is faster and more effective than any other means of media. People in the next county will know who did what in your church.

This will be exacerbated by the fact that, because it deals with low population numbers, the rural church must incorporate a multitude of ideas, theological fads, and socioeconomic groups into one unit if it is to have sufficient resources to minister at all!

Positive Perspectives. The rural "sense of community" can work well toward helping to accomplish the ministry of Christ, where there is "neither Jew nor Greek, slave nor free, male nor female." To generate sufficient numbers for vital ministry, the rural church must be inclusive. The rural church must be in touch with or minister to, in some manner, a very large percentage of its community, while the urban church need connect with only a fraction of one percent. While the urban church can afford to be homogeneous, the rural church must be heterogeneous.

Often the church is the last surviving community institution in a rural town. While inclusion and tolerance ought to be our aim in all ministry, the smaller numbers of rural demographics make it a must. The fact that rural people *want* to be a community is a plus in ministry. Fewer numbers to work with may mean less "age-grading"; parents and young people alike may be needed to produce a volleyball game. The result can be less genera- tion gap. The tolerance and inclusion necessary for successful ministry are compatible with true Christian values.

URBAN EXPECTATIONS

Negative Considerations. There is no rural minister who has not endured listening to a returning parishioner extol the wonders of a large, prosperous, urban church he or she recently visited. Given the demographics, econom- ics, and cultural conditioning of the rural congregation, the minister will surely run aground if he or she buys into too much urbania. There are some things you just cannot do in rural areas; however, that will not stop people from suggesting that you try!

At the beginning of his career, hotel entrepreneur Conrad Hilton tried to launch his business in the small town of Cisco, Texas. Hilton's mother, Mary, brought him to his senses when she said, "Conrad, if you want to launch a big ship you need to go where the water is deep." Rural congrega- tions need to come to grips with the fact that they are not situated on the "population ocean front." Perhaps, if your heart is set on launching a big ship, rural ministry is not for you!

Positive Perspectives. If you try to urbanize too much, you may lose your rural advantage. When families move to your area to escape urbania, define what it is that attracted them to the country or small village in the first place. Once defined, build these attractions into your church program. However, don't be surprised to find that these urban folk bring a great deal of urbania with them. Your challenge as a minister is to help these seeking people find what they are looking for in the rural worship experience, while at the same time incorporating the experience and skills they bring into the progress of the congregation.

THRESHOLD OF MINISTRY

Negative Considerations. In low-population areas, if church activities become too age graded or gender specific, numbers will not be sufficient to reach the *threshold of ministry*. There is the old story about the farmer who arrived at church to find that he and the minister were the only ones present. When the minister asked him what he wanted to do, the farmer replied, "If I had only one cow that showed up at feeding time, I'd feed her." The minister preached his sermon. On the way out the farmer said, "If only one cow showed up, I wouldn't give her the whole load." Every preacher knows that it is much more difficult to preach to a few people. Some activities require a certain *threshold number* in order to work at all.

Positive Perspectives. Congregations must be made aware of their own demographic profile, which should include population density, topography, age distribution, climate (climates that produce bad winter roads impact on ministry), and location of the church building. Realistic expectations must be generated from these facts. A midweek Bible study and prayer meeting of eight or 10 people will work very well, unless the congregation is expecting 30 to show up!

THE RURAL CHURCH IS MORE EFFECTIVE
THAN PEOPLE REALIZE

Several years ago I visited a large Lancaster County city church. The church boasted a membership of over 2,000 people. On the day I attended, worshipers numbered about 700, which I was told was a normal crowd.

The church had 10 full-time, paid employees. Upon looking at their annual financial statement, I discovered that our rural church is able to serve more congregants per employee for less money, our building expenses were much lower per member, and our missions giving was much higher per congregant. I suspect many rural churches would discover the same thing. While the numbers are not as big, the rural church does give a generous return on every ministry dollar!

Since our children do grow up, move away, then serve in urban congregations, perhaps we ought to consider things in a different light. Is it really so bad to produce Christian workers to serve Christ in urban areas? We rural churches must consider it part of our ministry to Christ. The rural church has indeed produced great numbers of workers for the urban church.

I know that is sometimes a bitter pill to swallow; yet there is a happier part to this. Here in the Austinville congregation, the hearts of those who have moved away to urban jobs are never far from us. Why? Because we've got the rural advantage! We're the *home* church. Two weeks ago we had couples and individuals home from Maryland, New Jersey, southern Pennsylvania, New York State, and the Ohio border. It feels great to see the kids! They're hard at work in churches all over the country.

Last month I had to send Dan and Holly's membership letter to an urban church in New Jersey. It was hard for me to get up the courage to write and send the letter. When I dropped it in the mail, I felt as if I were losing part of myself. They were "back home" this week and Holly sang a special number. On the way out of church they said, "Don't worry, we will always belong here." Then Jenny, who was back home from New York state, gave Gloria and me a big hug and said, "Boy, it sure seems good to be back home in this church again."

Originally published in The Five Stones *(Summer 1994), pp. 2-5; used by permission.*

Chapter 19

HOW CAN A SMALL CHURCH GROW?

Carl S. Dudley

The small, single-cell church behaves like an extended family in many ways. There are levels of participation, and latitude for individual characters. Members contribute to the whole, yet have a life apart from it. The most natural growth for the small church is *family style*, by birth and by adoption. Unfortunately, the young people who have been "born into" the small church often leave the community when they become young adults. Some will return; many will not.

Adoption, the other way for families to grow naturally, is one way by which the outsider becomes part of the family of God. According to the Apostle Paul, "adoption" is the means of acceptance central to Romans (chap. 8) and Galatians (chap. 4), and already assumed in Ephesians (chap. 1). But adoption is also implied throughout the New Testament, from the Synoptic Gospels and John through Revelation.

In adoption, the newcomer joins the history of the family. He or she cannot make a unilateral decision to join, cannot work his or her way into the family, to achieve belonging. Membership in the small church is a shared experience, based on a common faith and mutual understandings. The new member's faith statement must be mingled with the congregation's story-history. The adopted member of the church must learn to appreciate the family's artifacts and traditions, the annual feasts and perennial threats, and the secrets of their history. It takes time to adopt a child, and the whole family must participate.

The adopted member looks in a direction opposite to that of those joining the smaller group of a larger church. The latter member accepts the goals and purposes of the activity or interest group as part of the whole church. In the larger church, the new members join in creating a common future. But adoption begins by looking to the past. The adopted member joins the family history and must absorb the church, just as the church absorbs the new member.

Adoption depends on mutual respect and understanding. It cannot be rushed. It cannot be earned. Adopted members are often around the congregation for a long time before they "become members."

Most small churches cannot easily adopt new members, because they have been encouraged to neglect their history. Since adoption involves the congregation's pride in its own story of Christian witness, the members must feel that their history is worthy to be shared. Small churches which adopt members have a distinct sense that they have something to offer: a tradition of caring which is worth continuing. Often the history of the small church has roots in a particular place and is symbolized by significant objects. Growth by adoption can occur when the church feels good about its place of worship, and points with pride to the symbols of its past. Church cemeteries and pewter chalices can be as conducive to church growth as a highway location and a large Sunday school.

In small congregations, there are two particularly important functions that are essential to the process of adoption, and that may be performed by several people. One is the gatekeeper, and the other is the patriarch (or matriarch).

The gatekeepers linger around the edge of church meetings and congregational worship. They are often older, often male. Although they usually do not have positions of leadership, they enjoy greeting everyone, especially visitors. They like to know everyone and everything, but avoid the center of events. One pastor reports that they "go outside during the sermon, just to talk." Gatekeepers are important in the process of growth, interpreting the church to prospective members because they enjoy the contact. If they like the match of church and visitor, adoption is possible.

The patriarchs and matriarchs are at the center of the church. They sit in the center of the sanctuary and feel in the center of the congregation. They may have money and many friends, or they may have passed their prime. They may be friendly or aloof (one pastor describes a matriarch as "gruff on the outside, but a very caring person"). Patriarchs and matriarchs have one essential feature: they have lived through the history of the church. Carrying the church identity in their presence, they remember when things were different and "how we got to where we are."

Many young pastors consider patriarchs and matriarchs irrelevant antiquarians, but in the process of adoption they are essential. The "informal elders" who accept the new members, they complete the process by sharing the church history with the adoptees. New members know they are embraced by the church when they have been told the stories by the family's "elders." To be accepted, new members must appreciate the stories they have heard and the people who have told them. When that time comes, the covenant is shared.

Growth by adoption takes much longer than growth by division. In adoption, the new member joins the place as well as the people, and he or she must learn the beat of the music and the rhythm of the seasons. Task-oriented groups of larger congregations will assimilate newcomers more efficiently. But for those people who assimilate more slowly, adoption is the natural process, and the small church is the natural place.

The small church has grown, and it can't grow. It can be transformed, but not without losing the satisfactions of its smallness. And the small church can grow without changing, by adopting new members into the family. The number of new members may not be overwhelming, but the congregation can continue as an effective agency of God's love for those people in that place.

Previously published in Action Information *vol. 4, no. 1 (March 1978): pp. 6-7. Reprinted by permission from the* Christian Ministry *(July 1977); copyright © 1977, The Century Foundation.*

Chapter 20

EFFECTIVE APPROACHES TO GROWTH AND STEWARDSHIP IN THE SMALL CHURCH

Perry Bell

What makes small churches unique? And what special approaches to growth and stewardship are most effective in the small church? Pastors who want to develop these areas of their ministries may find it helpful to understand what makes this size of congregation distinctive.

Unlike larger churches, which often focus on tasks, smaller churches tend to uphold relationships as paramount and members tend to relate to one another as in a large family. Decisions about tasks or jobs are considered secondary and are often made in the church parking lot, amid exchanges of greetings and gossip.

The role of the minister differs, too. The pastor in a large church is a rather distant, powerful symbol whose role is to articulate the church's vision. In a small church, he or she is embraced as one of the family, but doesn't necessarily speak for that family.

This relational orientation of small churches is compelling in many ways. The small church provides a *network* of intimacy, a close-knit community that embraces its members and joins them together, providing a space even for the "odd" characters among them. As a result, members respond directly and personally when one of them is hurting or in need, sharing responsibility for what needs to be done.

Such mutual caring unifies the small church. Other factors also serve this same purpose. For instance, the small church has a strong sense of physical place. Objects assume a sacred significance. The pews, for example, hold a storehouse of tales about those who have filled them over the years. The church's windows may be dedicated to the memory of past members. These and other sacred objects in the church provide a sense of history and continuity. While this is also true in larger churches, in smaller congregations the communal memory is often stronger, as people are closer to the traditions, or have intimate knowledge of those to whom these objects are dedicated.

It is this common history, or shared past, that claims a central place in the small church. Members honor and remember those who have left their mark, from the initial visionaries and organizers to the socializers, including the jokesters and grumblers, who kept the place going and oiled the relationships. And they fondly recall the "saints" who had to work with them. (A living saint is one who has been around long enough to he able to say "But we *haven't* always done it that way!")

Trusted leaders also bind the small congregation together. Very often the real spiritual leader of the community is a layperson. I remember when I was young and green and had been in my first parish only about two years. We conducted a survey asking the congregation whom it most trusted for spiritual leadership, and Horace Thompson, a 75-year-old layman, won by a long shot. Needless to say, this was tough for me, the church's ordained minister, to accept. Horace was a quiet but solid kind of guy, with all the qualities of a saint. He led the adult Sunday School and helped with services. He was somebody whom I relied on and I came to accept the fact that others did, too. In this instance it was okay, even appropriate, to let Horace serve as the congregation's spiritual guide.

Annual events are another guiding and unifying influence in small churches. At many Wisconsin churches, autumn harvest festivals are commonplace, with people contributing pies, breads, and other baked goods. It has been my experience that people who never showed up in church on Sunday would participate, too. Sharing in their own way, joking and swapping tales, as though they'd always been around. The fringe members were brought together with the rest of the church community and reminded that they still belonged. In this way, annual happenings play an important role in defining congregations.

Even conflict has its proper place in the small church. A certain amount of conflict is a measure of the closeness of a congregation, and some inherent hostilities hold a church together. Bickering is partly how the community conducts its business and is not to be confused with dislike.

The Challenge to Growth in the Small Church

Christ commanded his followers to "go make disciples!" But how do you lay the foundation for increasing membership in small, tightly bonded churches?

Clearly, this kind of church, like a family, treasures its time-honored traditions and its rituals. Yet often the traditions and closeness mask problems related to growth. Small congregations often have a self-image problem: Because their church is small, they don't believe they are worthy, but perceive themselves as weak, unattractive, and powerless, with a limited future. Certainly, the institution, like an individual with low self-esteem, is not prone to reach out warmly to embrace others. This withholding is usually not conscious. But it is important for ministers to help congregations examine how they feel about themselves and to address such institutional attitudes before forcing them to welcome others into their midst.

In this and other ways, the minister plays a key role in helping a small church grow. Research, in fact, confirms that growth in the small church is unlikely to be stimulated by existing membership, but rests mostly with the pastor. Often churches will say, "We want our church to grow," but really don't mean it. Acceptance of newcomers into the life and ministry of a church often carries a price that the old-timers are unwilling to pay. It means they would have to give up some power, share some of the minister's time and energy with others, and adjust to change. It means they would have to deal with not knowing "who all those people are." (After all, "stranger" means danger in a small community, and newer people almost always are seen as a threat.)

Given the reluctance of at least some in any congregation to take on such changes willingly, what should a minister do? A pastor can help the congregation focus on their qualms about all of this, holding discussions with members to help them honestly and prayerfully consider how they feel about bringing in new people. Do we want to grow? Why or why not? Do we really mean it? What does growth mean to us personally? What will it mean to the church? How do we reach out to new people?

Evangelism only works when a congregation is clear about the answers to these questions. Equally important, and perhaps more so, is a church's dedication to its mission to be the church. Talk about growth is meaningless if the church itself has not identified its mission and role in the world. If a congregation is deeply supportive of its members and involved within the community and beyond, then others will see this and be drawn to it. Those who are living out the gospel as the center of their existence and teaching discipleship by example act as a powerful magnet. Growth simply happens when the word gets out that this is a powerfully committed group of people.

This does not mean abandoning time-honed traditions or giving up those aspects of the church that impart a sense of belonging. It means an openness to sharing these communal "treasures" with others, and even encouraging the development of new groups for new members to join in. It means reaching out consciously to those who are "outsiders" and inviting them to join in. It means giving the minister support and allowing him or her the time to develop contacts and reach out to potential new members, rather than just attending to existing membership. And it requires sensitivity and good communication—continuing to make time for the congregation to talk about the disruptions caused by growth, which undoubtedly has caused some discomfort while maintaining the vision of outreach.

If the small church is "family," then the family grows through adoption, through the inviting of others to enter into these old traditions and to become part of the supportive church community and its mission. Let me give you an example. About 20 years ago, I was the minister of a United Methodist church of about 75 people in rural, south-central Wisconsin. Since this was a region dominated by Catholic and Lutheran churches, we Methodists were perhaps a bit more flexible or open to new members than those more established institutions. Some of our church members began to operate a food pantry for the rural poor and, as part of this task, decided to take special care of one particularly needy family. Today, nearly two decades later, members of that family still play an active part in that church. This is what happens when we are simply doing what we are supposed to be doing.

STEWARDSHIP ISSUES IN THE SMALL CHURCH

Just as issues related to small-church growth can be knotty, so can those related to stewardship. This is an especially difficult arena in rural churches, where farmers have experienced skyrocketing expenses coupled with drastically declining returns on their investments over the last few decades, and where families are struggling just to make ends meet. Appealing for money is a complicated process, and in most small congregations it is a particularly sensitive issue. Because of the uncertainty of income and the need to scrounge, the church treasurer frequently takes on a conservative or protective stance that quenches enthusiasm for new programs or denominational funding. Many members resist pledging, making budget planning difficult.

Despite appearances to the contrary, however, money is almost never the immediate issue. Stewardship is more a question of will and motivation. Usually there is another need involved, and that need lifting up—helping the congregation see it and deal with it—often solves the problem. I recently served a congregation that never had any money to give. But one Tuesday the church roof was damaged by high winds. By the following Sunday, unbeknownst to me, the parishioners had raised $5,000 and had seen to it that the roof was completely redone. It was a clear case of the need having been lifted up and met. In a crisis, the will and motivation to give took over, and the money manifested itself.

This example proves another point: If stewardship appeals can be made personal, related to individuals, to immediate crises, or to the place and life the church community shares, members will be more open. Giving can actually be fun when you know who or what you're giving to.

And sometimes the generosity of congregations is an inspiration. Flooding disasters in the upper Midwest in the past decade offer a prime example. Small rural congregations contributed significant amounts of money for flood relief. For instance, in 1991 one such church sustained more than $1,000 in flood damage to its own buildings, yet collected and sent more than $1,400 to help others, again proving the point that money is rarely the issue.

When there appears no church-related crisis or personal need to appeal to, ministers and church leaders may want to encourage the congregation to use regular church events, such as the autumn harvest festival, as church fundraisers. New events can be organized for this purpose, involving the entire congregation and serving both as stewardship and growth opportunities.

Sometimes, in particularly dire circumstances, it may be necessary to appeal to the broader town or village in which the church is located. Small communities value their churches for the traditions and values they stand for, and most townsfolk are willing to help if a church's very survival is at issue.

Sometimes stewardship requires utterly practical approaches. For example, you might post a "wish list" of items the church needs. Sunday school supplies, a microwave for the kitchen, renovated bathrooms—these sorts of things can help people see a specific need to which they can give. And you might also suggest planned giving—wills, bequests, memorials. These can provide a standing fund that can help alleviate the necessity of scraping along from one financial crisis to the next.

Whether addressing evangelism or stewardship concerns, certainly a minister who has the gift for caring is critical to all aspects of small-church life. A caring pastor knows the names of parishioners, spends time with them over meals or coffee, visits in their homes, and ministers to them when they are sick or in need. Such a minister creates meaningful worship services and honors regular fellowship times. He or she calls the church together for things other than money, becoming involved in activities such as church retreats and mission projects. A minister who is highly participatory, effective, and faithful in his or her calling will find a small church responsive to this dedication and will reap the rewards in church growth and sound financial stewardship.

Originally published in Congregations: The Alban Journal *20, no. 5 (September/October 1994): pp. 9-11.*

Chapter 21

No Church Door Is Completely Open: Making Inclusion Work

Kenneth R. Marple

A ll churches want new people to come, while at the same time they effectively keep them out. It may not be as easy to get into your church as you may think. While our primary concern has always been "how to *get* people in, "the real challenge may be "how to *let* them in." If you think the doors to your church are completely open—think again!

"Most churches and religious organizations attract and absorb people who are very much like those who are already members," says Leith Anderson in his book *Dying For Change.*[1] Anderson continues by saying, "Basically there are two types of churches. One is the church that establishes systems to attract and incorporate persons who are different. Both have risks. People who are different will change the church; people who are the same will keep the church from changing."

WHAT KEEPS PEOPLE OUT OF YOUR CHURCH?

"Push" and "pull" are the two components of every decision to fellowship with a given church or not. All churches have characteristics, histories, and community images that serve to push some folk away, while pulling others in. The "pulls" of other churches combined with the "pushes" of your church could translate into empty pews.

Twenty years ago, when my wife, Gloria, and I came to minister at our present rural church, there was a rusty stovepipe that ran up the front of the building, the church needed painting, there were no sidewalks, and parking was on the muddy rutted lawn surrounding the church. On our first Sunday I got covered with mud while helping to push out a stuck car after the service. In addition, the 30- by 40-foot building was too small to accommodate weddings that are often attended by 200-300 guests. There was, of course, no handicap access, and the church provided no services to the community. While there was no sign to tell passers-by what the church was all about, the visual sign clearly said, "private property, keep out." The church had poor access.

Yet, church doors are effectively kept shut to the public by a more insidious barricade. Our church is located in the country about six miles from the service town. Recently, while visiting with a couple who started attending soon after we arrived, we learned that when they first moved into the area, they were invited to an elite town church and told that if they attended our small country church, they would not be accepted in the community. As it turned out, they couldn't be more accepted by our regional community! The stories are out there. I grew up in the Dutch Neck Presbyterian Church, so when the movie *A River Runs Through It* came out I was eager to see it, since it was about a Presbyterian minister and his two boys. I remember one of the Presbyterian boys, when talking about the Methodists, said, "Dad always said that Methodists are just Baptists who can read." Since I'm now a Baptist minister, the joke hit a little hard.

The truth is, how wide the church doors swing open is affected more than it should be by the socioeconomic level, and the class aspirations of folk on either side of your church doors. There is a certain sadness in realizing that the fall of television minister Jimmy Bakker was rooted deeply in this ugly concept. Bakker felt "put down" by others as he grew up in the church. He had strong feelings about being thought of as "second class." When Bakker told his board, "We're going first class," he was caught up in a class struggle that has never served the church well. Jesus taught us to beware of the Scribes and the Pharisees—"They love to have the place of honor at banquets and the best seats in the synagogue" (Matthew 23:6). Many times, our own attempts to distance ourselves from a lower socioeconomic world is rooted in our own feelings of inferiority.

The factors that keep people out of the church are often completely unknown to the minister. The kinds of things that close the door of our church to segments of the community are as strange as an affair that occurred 50 years ago and a neighborhood feud that occurred 30 years ago! Small churches are often in small communities with deeply entrenched populations, as compared to typical urban populations. These people have known one another for a hundred years, and that may turn out to be your biggest problem. Who will sit in church with whom may go back a long time.

I've had times when church attendance dropped off sharply, only to discover that the town itself was in a conflict that divided it into two factions, or that a large family was in the middle of a feud. Other things that will form a sure-fire barrier between certain individuals in the community will be a divorce, sexism, and racism. There are often barriers that the minister may never know about, such as spouse abuse or sexual abuse. All of these things are invisible barriers that keep folk from walking through the seemingly open doors to your church.

INCLUSION IS AN OPEN-DOOR CONCEPT

Heart disease appears to strike suddenly. In truth, its causes are subtly at work underneath for many years. So it is when the church fails to embrace Christ's teaching of inclusion—poor health or even death results from a lack of heart toward all people. A wide-open church door has more to do with inclusion than with any other single issue.

Having grown up in the 1940s and early 1950s in the migrant farm country of central New Jersey, many of my friends were African American. We played together, ate together, went to school together, and visited one another's homes. Still, as I grew older I gained an awareness of some sort of invisible line between whites and blacks. There was no civil-rights movement, the NAACP was a mere fledgling, and Rosa Parks and Martin Luther King, Jr., were virtually unknown.

In our Sunday school we sang, "Jesus loves the little children, all the children of the world. Red and yellow, black and white, they are precious in his sight. Jesus loves the little children of the world." By singing that little song we seemed to assure ourselves that we were fair and loving people, who held bias toward none. Then in 1954 my family and I took a trip to Miami to visit Aunt Delores and Uncle Eddy. As we moved deeper into the south I began to see signs on the restaurants that announced "whites only" or "no colored." All of the restrooms and drinking fountains were labeled either *white* or *colored*. There seemed to be a special door for everyone. It was the concrete block wall that riveted my attention. In the city of Miami there was a miles-long, concrete block wall, like the Great Wall of China— only junky, that separated the black part of the city from the white part. People simply called it "the colored section."

The trip that was intended to be about palm trees, alligators, fishing, Lake Okeechobee, Seminole Indians, and the Everglades, turned out to be about a wall. I knew about the invisible wall, it's just that I had never seen it spelled out so clearly in black and white only. Yet, invisible or concrete and steel, both are real, both are meant to exclude—so much for "Red and yellow, black and white, they are precious in his sight."

It was 1966; racial violence erupted in Dayton, Chicago, Atlanta, and San Francisco. I was beginning my first pastorate in a tiny Washington state logging and fishing village. In our village, the violence was only something to talk about. Anyway, we weren't biased—no walls in our town. The town itself looked a lot like Cicely on the television show *Northern Exposure*. That morning I had a nice visit on the sidewalk with Bertha Hollaway, a logger's wife—she said she and the boys would be coming to church! The phone rang as I entered the house; it was Lolly Gibble with a message for me: "If you want to stay here, you had better not be seen on the street talking with that woman again." Lolly moved in the upper levels of the little town's societal system, and she intended that her church would too. After all, her husband was in management, and she had been to college. There was that confounded wall again. This time it was keeping people out of the church.

If real life imitates television, then Lolly Gibble was my Cora Beth Godsey (of *The Waltons* fame), or Harriet Olsen (of *Little House on the Prairie* fame). While your church may not be on Walton's Mountain or in Walnut Grove, the greatest block to total access to your church will not be the church building; it will be Lolly Gibble, or Cora Beth Godsey, or Harriet Olsen standing at the church door to welcome some warmly and turn away others politely. The decision I made after that phone call was pivotal to all my future ministry—I decided that I would try to keep both Lolly and Bertha in the church.

Today, *inclusion* is still only a fledgling concept within many churches. We generally think of it in terms of ramps, elevators, curb cuts, and noble tolerance. As part of a committee interviewing applicants for an administrative position in our school district, I listened to numerous applicants explain the concept of inclusion in terms of access for the handicapped. Then one particularly insightful applicant came along and explained it in terms of *access for everyone*, regardless of race, ethnic background, gender, or socioeconomic situation. This kind of inclusion involves the heart as well as the body.

GETTING INCLUSION TO WORK:
OPENING THE CHURCH DOOR A LITTLE WIDER

Inclusion is a healing concept. The Bible teaches inclusion when it says, "There is no longer Jew or Greek, there is no longer slave or free, there is no longer male or female; for all of you are one in Christ Jesus" (Galatians 3:28). In order for the entire community to gain access to your church, the covert, invisible barriers need to be removed from the path that leads to your church door. It is a cinch that the folk who are effectively outside are not going to knock the door down, so you must work with those already inside to get them to swing open the church doors from the inside. I like to think of the words and ministry of Christ as healing. For the church, inclusion must mean taking Christ seriously. More than ever, the church is polarized on a myriad of issues, yet the saving ground of the church has always been the healing words of Christ. Christ said, "Listen ! I am standing at the door, knocking; if you hear my voice and open the door, I will come into you and eat with you, and you with me" (Revelation 3:20). The first step to inclusion may well be to let the consoling, healing, forgiving spirit of Christ inside. It was, after all, Christ who said, "And I, when I am lifted up from the earth, will draw *all people* to myself" (John 12:32).

Good preaching must heal hearts; as hearts are healed so are communities. There is an elderly Methodist minister who remains a cherished friend of mine. Over his long career he has risen to great heights in the Methodist conference; yet his advice to me has always been shockingly simple: "Ken, don't get too far to the left or too far to the right; make sure that you stay pretty much to the center—Christ and the cross." Be sure to preach a lot of forgiveness, humility, and humanity. Preaching is still the greatest power of the minister (1 Corinthians 1:21). Preaching sets the tone and standard, creating the spiritual climate that people are bound to operate in. We may think our preaching makes little difference, but when we preach the Sermon on the Mount people know they have heard a standard of caring, forgiveness, humility, and tolerance, that will result in a spirit of *inclusion* that cannot be debated.

As sermons are prepared, you might want to think about including two or more storylines in your sermon. After all, there are teachers, farmers, blue-collar workers, young and old listening. Not all of these people will be listening for the same things. By putting in separate storylines for the academic, the theology buff, and the pragmatist, you will effectively open the church doors to a broader spectrum of your community. In this manner, you can send everyone home with different sermons that deliver the same message.

The pastor must use his or her influence to assure that church leaders are door openers! Next to the pastor, the church is known by its leaders. The fostering of forgiveness and humility will do just to open the church doors a little wider than any other thing. Years ago, an aggressive, arrogant man moved to our community. He quickly aspired to the office of deacon, threatening to leave our church with his family (and friends) if he was not given some power. Graciously, an older farmer resigned his post to make room for the man on our board. It turned out to be the worst fiasco the church has ever endured. By way of contrast, I remember asking an old retired carpenter if he would be willing to serve as a deacon in our church; he responded with tears as he said, "Oh, I could never do that; I'm not worthy." Needless to say, he made the best deacon the church has ever had. Humility opens church doors to the community; arrogance closes them.

Pastoral visits can open church doors. Early in my ministry, Norman Vincent Peale set the tone for all my pastoral visiting. Peale used to tell the story of a conflict that divided the community in his first church. The conflict was rooted in just two women who, many years before, had a disagreement that led to their separation. Peale was invited to eat a slice of pie at the home of one of these women. When he commented on how good the pie was, the woman replied that she was never able to make pie as good as the other woman. Peale soon visited the other woman, taking this compliment to her. The two women were brought back together and the church doors were opened a little wider! So, in pastoral visits, make it a point to deliver not only the Good News, but also "good news."

While no church door is completely open, it is the minister's job to continually work at dismantling the invisible barriers that effectively block access to the church. Over three decades ago, on the day that Lolly Gibble called, I made a choice that I would try to hang onto both Lolly Gibble and Bertha Hollaway. Years later, when I left that church, Lolly had dismantled all but the lower part of her elitist wall. At a logging company dinner, sitting across from Bertha Hollaway, Lolly was overheard to say, "It seems so good to associate with the *common workers' wives once in a while.*" Lolly was making progress. At any rate, when I left the church I still had both Lolly and Bertha. The bottom line is clear: if we could open the church doors to just the people who have no problems, there would be no one at all to come in—but then, if that were the standard, they wouldn't have a minister anyway.

NOTE

1. Leith Anderson, *Dying for Change* (Minneapolis: Bethany House, 1990).

Originally published in The Five Stones *(Summer 1995), pp. 2-6; used by permission.*

Chapter 22

EVANGELISM AND TOMORROW'S SMALL CHURCH

Anthony G. Pappas

My perspective on the church scene in North America is admittedly limited, but I believe it represents reality. What I see doesn't excite me very much. Like the children of Israel on the banks of the Red Sea, the only way forward would appear to be via miraculous intervention. Well, maybe that is where the church should be.

Evangelism is the sharing of good news, or, as attributed to D. T. Niles, one beggar telling another where the bread is. If God fills our souls, as bread fills a beggar's tummy, we ought not have too much trouble at least making good news noises. However, we have fine-tuned a form of evangelism that is not particularly good news and is clearly not effective any longer. There are at least seven strategies for evangelism that, though they no longer work well or at all, we insist upon using.

WHAT DOESN'T BRING PEOPLE TO CHRIST OR CHRIST'S BODY

1. *Duty.* One ought to go to church. Maybe so, but as an effective motivator this one went out with hula-hoops. Duty, loyalty, self-sacrifice for the good of the whole, honor, institutional maintenance—not only do these not motivate, they are perceived to be psychologically harmful!

2. *Guilt.* The majority of the population today possess one of two kinds of consciences. Some are nonfunctioning, so there is no point in trying to make these people feel bad about not being a Christian. (Pardon a theological intrusion here, but this is a humdinger of a strategy—evangelizing so that bad news may abound!) Then there are those with over-sensitive consciences—these folks are already in church (but they can't evangelize

because they don't live the good news) or they are already in therapy and aren't about to risk their multithousand-dollar investment to this appeal!

3. *Open Doors.* "If you build it, they will come" is the catchphrase of the movie *Field of Dreams*. It is also the evangelism strategy of a whole generation. Build a big new building and society will just pour people in. Amazingly, this worked for a decade or two, but no longer. Just being there will no longer do it. Alban Institute founder Loren Mead has noted correctly: the church is not even a blip on the current generation's radar screen!

4. *Family Tradition or Expectations.* The 20-somethings do almost nothing the way their parents do: music, food, lifestyle, marriage, work, and so forth. So it shouldn't be surprising that they don't do church either. The graying of mainline North American churches gives mute testimony to this fact.

5. *Fear of Hell* or (for that matter) *Hope of Heaven*. The majority of the population feel that heaven and hell are here-and-now realities. The "good news" that through faith in Jesus they can avoid a toasty afterlife is not motivating. The promise of a future heaven or hell just does not carry the same psychological power that it did even a generation ago. We are so used to beating this horse, we failed to note that it has died!

6. *Coercion.* High-pressure tactics, buttonholing, intimidation, and bullying is ineffective. Zeal is no substitute for love. Thanks be to God that this strategy no longer has the impact it once did. All (except, unfortunately, those with significant pathologies) just walk away.

7. *Formalism/Traditionalism.* For some amazing reason, people will endure mindless, heartless rituals, if they are *their* rituals. I know few people who care to sit through an hour of boring nonsense that belongs to somebody else (by the way, to whom do our worship forms belong anyhow? Grandpa? Great-great-great-grandpa?) For 20 years as a small-church pastor I vowed that everyone who gave the hour of our church worship service would leave uplifted. To whatever measure the Holy Spirit granted success, we poured some new wine into those old wineskins. Now I wonder if it wasn't a wrong-headed enterprise to begin with. In my position as an area minister I visit a different church every week. Often I leave asking, Would a visitor ever come back? The service is entirely passive; the music

antique; the liturgy disconnected from life. And even if, in my view, the content of the sermon redeems the hour, nevertheless the form is anti-quated, monological, and slow in a fast-paced, interactive world. I have no doubt that God can save the world, but I wonder if even God can save us from ourselves.

"Well," you are thinking, "you acid-tongued cynic, just what would you propose?" I wish I had an ironclad program to revitalize our churches and share good news. I don't. We must all wait on the Holy Spirit. Maybe an international day of repentance, fasting, and prayer would help. In the mean-time, simply to stimulate our thinking, I offer some goals and strategies.

WHAT MIGHT ATTRACT PEOPLE TO CHRIST AND CHRIST'S BODY?

1. *Life, Energy, Dynamism.* Once my family and I were leaving a worship service where we had been visitors. I had my own reactions, but I slapped a smile on my face and, with a jolly lilt to my voice, asked my teenagers how they liked the service. "In a word, Dad, BORING." My kids have also considered carnivals and history-changing battlefields boring, so their re-sponse didn't trouble me. What bothered me was that I couldn't, on the basis of the hour we had just experienced, argue against their conclusion. They were right. Christians should leave worship energized, excited, enthu-siastic for having touched the living God. What are we doing wrong? For starters we have a poor theology (and practice) of the Spirit. We consider the Holy Spirit to be given to the individual upon his or her faith response. We have forgotten to operate on the truth that the Spirit is given to the church; it is the Spirit that quickens the Body of Christ. Spiritual energy can flow when many people share their insights, experiences, and emotions and the Holy Spirit builds upon those gifts, it is not entertainment that is the antidote for boredom; it is involvement in the substance of spiritual life.

2. *Points of Salvation.* Protestant history, especially in North America, includes much in the way of revivals and revivalism—salvation seen as a total and emotional experience. Once having "got religion," folk subsequently "got respectable." Then salvation became a rigid adherence to a righteous lifestyle defined by the moralism of the day. Somehow we need to get beyond these two inadequate conceptualizations of salvation and reclaim

the divine power to save us. So I offer a goal of evangelism under the rubric, *points of salvation*. This simply means that an enterprise of evangelism is to discern a point at which our neighbor is hurting and then to channel God's healing touch. This might lead us to be active in building such points of salvation as 12-step groups, anger workshops, retirement planning seminars, first-time mother classes, budgeting basics, and so forth. Of course, none of these—or even all of these together—are the whole gospel. They are only points of salvation, but I wonder if this approach might not get us a whole lot further than our current practice of salvation without a point.

3. *Spirituality.* "Bible-baseball darts?" I echoed incredulously. "Yes sir," the successful pastor of my father's generation affirmed. "Every church I went to started a vibrant men's group playing Bible-baseball darts!" Darts, painting the sanctuary, sitting on a committee—I don't believe these will do it anymore. People are looking for spiritual nourishment. There is a craving for inner strengthening, relational health, and meaning in work and leisure activities. Every shrinking church I visit laments the secularization and spiritual disinterest of society. At the very same time books such as Scott Peck's *The Road Less Traveled* and Thomas Moore's *Care of the Soul* have become best-sellers and remain so for months on end. People are spiritually hungry, starving even. The difference is they are no longer willing to collude with the church in an avoidance of inner work and inner issues. They no longer see the point in maintaining a form of godliness that denies the power of that God. Society's rejection of traditional "churchianity" is God's call to reclaim the spirituality of our faith. I am still convinced that if we offer spiritual resources, if we live into spiritual realities, they will come. People will always need what the Holy Spirit has to offer, but they won't settle for the wrapping paper anymore.

4. *Benefit.* People will respond to those things that bring them a blessing. Jesus "for the joy set before Him endured the cross" (Heb. 12:2). Most churches are very quick to load crosses on the backs of their current or prospective members, but very slow in delivering any joy. Churches that call people who seek to be blessed "unspiritual" are trading the joy of God's presence for the self-defeating satisfactions of judgmentalism. Society has many dynamics in operation that suck the spiritual life out of people: the demands of jobs, rigorous and unrelenting schedules, the nagging of un- or under-fulfilled commitments. There is no one who needs yet another place

to be sucked dry. If the church cannot not be a place of refreshment, blessing, and benefit, then we ought to sell all that we have and give the money to the poor. We need to organize our congregational life so that people can say, deeply and sincerely, "It has been good to be in the house of the Lord!"

5. *A Sense of Purpose.* "Why am I here?" is the question each human being asks and answers with their life. The church has the blessed opportunity to offer God's answer, the one, true, and eternal answer, to those who are asking. The church of Jesus Christ is on a crusade for eternity. But keeping these church doors open because my great-grandma is buried out in the yard isn't a good strategy to keep the church alive. If we were following Christ's command to feed the hungry, visit the imprisoned, heal the sick, and give sight to the blind, people would join us and find meaning in their involvement.

STRATEGIES FOR SMALL-CHURCH EVANGELISM

1. *Starting New Small Churches through Marketing Techniques.* Many denominations are active in starting new churches. One, I understand, will fund only those new church starts that can be projected to have 500 members within five years. Their life as a small church is intended to be brief. Locations for these churches will be small in number and high in selectivity. Another denomination is projecting 500 new churches in a decade, the vast majority of which are anticipated to have bivocational leadership. These will start small and stay smallish. This denomination is trying to gear up their bivocational training programs. A third denomination utilizes a mass-marketing telephone campaign. They bring in a bank of telephones and telephoners and blitz the population with information about a new church. From this effort they expect a 1 percent response rate. With 20,000 calls, they will have enough to start a new church! Another denomination trains church planting pastors to make 10,000 house calls in one year. They expect a 2 percent response rate, which is low but enough to launch a new congregation. Two thoughts come to mind: First, these strategies are obviously limited to regions of at least 50,000 people. Second, who responds to such an appeal and how is the body of Christ built from such atomized beginnings? Maybe with time and experience we can learn more about the strengths and weaknesses of this strategy.

2. *Relational Networking.* We sat around the table in the church's Sunday School room. The Anglos present listened politely as the Hispanics went on and on about how the Lord was blessing them. They had started a couple of years earlier with little more than a roof over their heads, some concerned families from that city, and some families borrowed from a Hispanic church an hour away. From that handful, the congregation had grown to nearly 60 regular worshipers and 125 people at the last Family Sunday. "What's a Family Sunday?" I asked. This small, financially struggling, ethnic congregation so designates one Sunday a quarter. They prepare a potluck supper and invite all the members of their extended families, their friends and neighbors, and anybody else whom they bump into, to this special service. It is a service designed to make guests feel especially welcome as they present Christ's love to them in word and deed. Fellowship, family feeling, relational network recruiting, do-able schedule . . . hmmm, it seems there is a lesson here somewhere. Carl Dudley has said that a small church grows in the same way a family grows, by birth and by adoption (see chapter 18). Small-church evangelism is a relational enterprise. Small churches bring people to Christ by bringing them into the family of faith. It is not mass evangelism, but it is very effective evangelism when it is actually done and when the congregation is healthy. My colleague Duncan Mcintosh has developed diagnostic tools by which he feels he can predict the future of evangelistic efforts in a congregation by likening their dynamics to three types of families. The first congregation he calls constricted; they have collapsed on themselves and are often dysfunctional. This congregation has a net evangelistic effort that is negative; that is, they will be smaller in the days ahead. The second type of congregation he likens to a *nuclear family*, a family of siblings. This congregation will hold its own, more or less, gaining members in the range of its losses. The third type he likens to an *extended family*, a family of cousins, a family with plenty of "holes," spaces for new people to enter. This congregation will experience net positive evangelism in the days ahead. This model of small-church evangelism operates through the relationships of the congregation, welcoming others to Christ through their love. They develop significant transformative relationships, but in a social fabric that can "breathe."

3. *Community Center.* A small church in the town next to ours is proud, and well they should be. A few years ago they hovered on the brink of extinction. Their new pastor helped them channel their loving inclinations into specific community ministries. Now they house a senior daycare, numerous

12-step groups, food distributions, and so forth. Their pastor reports that one out of every two hours each day, day in and day out, their church building is in use serving the community's needs. This is a form of incarnational evangelism. So when a proclamational evangelism is added to it, the credibility is already earned for a true hearing. As long as our governments continue to distance themselves from the needy, opportunities for the church to serve can only grow. Will churches choose to incarnate evangelism? And can we learn to speak the redeeming word to these new people within our own walls?

4. *Structural Changes*. My position as an area minister sometimes takes me to two dozen churches in just two months' time. With some exceptions, I have come to see a pattern: Small churches are getting smaller, and what they are used to doing to remedy that situation is not working. I once listened for an hour as an elderly congregation recounted for me their efforts to attract new members. Valiant efforts they were, but unavailing. The fact is that people aren't buying what we are selling. (Some nostalgia buffs are, but not in sufficient quantities to re-people our empty pews.) And what we are selling is something less than the full gospel. It is our cultural version of the gospel, and though not invalid for us, it is ineffectual for most others. What is needed, of course, is a different culture or medium of expressing the Good News.

Two ways that this is occurring, though exceptional, are starting to emerge. The first is through *congregational death and resurrection*. Over a decade ago my denomination made a big push for new church starts, but leadership in the more highly churched areas created a category called "restart." These were attempts to pour new life into an older congregation that had begun to teeter on the brink. Findings showed that restarts seldom worked. The remnant congregation wanted new resources to chase their old dream. Much energy was expended demonstrating the passé nature of their style of Christianity. Fortunately, we wised up and now restarts are sanctioned after a congregation votes itself legally dead. A new group which is not seeking to replicate a specific past then attempts to envision a new ministry in that place.

The second structure *involves starting a new congregation out of the old one* (or, at least, a second worship service of a different culture). Small churches tend to have major problems with this concept, not only because it is so different, but also because of the need for social unity. The pastor of a church not many miles hence got a vision to start a Saturday evening worship service in a contemporary style, followed by a covered-dish supper, to complement the traditional Sunday morning service of worship. One year into the experiment 60 folk are regular attendees on Saturday afternoon, and the pastor is both energized and exhausted. The 40 Sunday morning worshipers are experiencing a range of emotions from joy to defensiveness! I am convinced that unless small congregations renounce themselves and start to bear the cross of an alternative service they will severely limit their ability to follow Christ and proclaim good news into the future. The exact nature of the new culture embodied in the second service will vary according to the social environment, the vision of the church, and the gifts God has given them to use.

5. *Being Church for the 21st Century.* New ways of incarnating the Good News, of being Christ's body are starting to become discernible as we peer into the mists of the future. These include catalysts, covenants, clusters, and coalitions. *Catalyst churches* have a different self-image then most churches currently have. They do not see themselves as the unique locus of God's activity, but rather as the connective tissue in the incarnation of a particular aspect of God's kingdom in their setting. Currently a mid- to large-sized church may decide to program to meet the parenting needs of some of its members. A small church might note the same needs but would likely despair of a positive response. A catalytic church, even a quite small one, would be energized by this window of opportunity. It might broker a local counseling agency, an amenable daycare center, and some funding from a service organization to host an eight-week parenting seminar. It would honor and be fair to the other sponsoring organizations, but would find positive ways to share its motivation: the experience of God's love embodied in addressing immediate needs. The catalytic church would likely remain small, lean and responsive, but have an impact disproportionately large. It would attract those who feel at home at the intersection of meaning and mission.

Covenant churches are groups of churches that commit themselves to mutual accountability and ministry. I know of a group of 12 such churches in a poor county in a rural state. Together they have conducted evangelism ministries, children's missions, an affordable housing program, an employment project, and food assistance. They have become a beacon of righteousness and hope in a sea of squalor and despair.

Clusters refers to a way of organizing a smaller group of churches so that they can offer the ministries of a trained, diverse staff, and exhibit high lay ownership in the local church. In a cluster, churches are each responsible for their own building, local budget, Sunday School, and so forth. Each then purchases pastoral services from a pool created by the cluster. So, for instance, five congregations, none of which could afford a full-time pastor, might together employ two full-time pastors, and part-time ministers of counseling, youth work, and music.

Cooperative churches, as the term is used here, is based on the richness of the divine nature and the pluralism of modem society. Instead of seeing the former as impractical theology and the latter as an evil to be opposed, cooperative churches attempt to organize on this basis. In one county six churches might elect to cooperate. One might be fundamentalistic in orientation, another traditional, another committed to spiritual direction as its form of faithfulness, another to one or more social ministries, another to finding contemporary expressions of the gospel, another to charismatic forms. Each would maintain their own pastor, meeting place, program, and internal life. Together they might share ministry in the areas of youth work, Vacation Bible School, choir(s), lay training, rallies, hands-on mission, camping, and so forth. Their uniqueness would lie in their commitment to evangelism. Each congregation would see itself as a feeder for all six congregations! Instead of competing with one another, cooperative churches would seek to find the right congregational home for each visitor who musters up the courage to cross a church threshold! Toothpaste manufacturers and restaurant chains are getting rich using such a strategy, it is inherent in Christ's gospel, but structurally churches continue to follow Adam Smith and Charles Darwin instead of Jesus Christ. It would take a whole new consciousness and level of team work among pastors, but greater miracles have happened.

***

We have explored some of the whys, why nots, and hows of evangelism today and into tomorrow. We need a whole new bunch of structures to implement tomorrow's evangelism. Mostly what we need are Christians whose faith fires their souls. *Lord we believe. Help thou our unbelief.* Amen.

Originally published in The Five Stones *(Spring 1997), pp. 2-7; used by permission.*

Part Four
THE SMALL CHURCH IN MISSION

Chapter 23

DEVELOPING STANDARDS
FOR
SMALL-CHURCH MISSION EVALUATION

Anthony G. Pappas

S mall-church mission. . . . hmmm. Sounds like an oxymoron, doesn't it? Oxymorons are different from other morons in that they are phrases which are intentionally contradictory. You know, like

- Jumbo shrimp
- Civil war
- Self-made Christian
- Controlled spontaneity
- Free trade
- Wedded bliss (or so my wife claims)

So the phrase "small-church mission" strikes many people as having two meanings that contradict each other. Small churches don't—can't—do mission.

A high-level executive in a mainline denomination once voted against a small grant to encourage renewal in his denomination's small churches. When asked why, he is quoted as saying, "What's the use? Small churches are only interested in surviving."

There are over one-third of a million congregations in our nation. About two-thirds of the churches in each denomination are categorized as "small." Therefore, there are over 200,000 small churches in our land, give or take 10,000 or so. It intrigues me that 200,000 gatherings of God's people can be dismissed in one phrase by a supposedly intelligent, sensitive, and faithful Christian leader.

And yet . . . don't we fear that he might be right?

From where that leader sits it appears that small churches expend precious resources and produce precious little mission output. Is this an objective assessment or an inherent bias in the bureaucratic perspective?

Is he failing to see mission activity by small churches because it is not there or because his filters block it from his vision?

Years ago two little boys in my community tragically suffocated to death, trapped inside an old-fashioned refrigerator. We were stunned and rallied around the distraught parents. The day before the funeral a reporter from the state's largest newspaper came to do a story on the community's response. He couldn't find any. Desperate for this "human interest" angle on the story, he came to see me, the pastor. How could I point him to the innumerable visits at homes, telephone contacts, casseroles delivered with love, shoulders cried on, and so forth? We operated in a different system, one that was invisible to his perspective.

In the same way, denominational structures operate differently than the small church. Theirs is a bureaucratic system, ours a tribal system. Often we are half-invisible to them, and they are half-incomprehensible to us. Unfortunately, value judgments are attached to these nonunderstandings.

It is inherent in the nature of bureaucracy to weigh the small church and find it wanting. The bureaucracy devalues the small church, not because the bureaucracy is evil, nor because the small church is lazy or unfaithful, but because they are two fundamentally different social structures. So different that they do not register each other for what each is. Rather, denominational structures and small churches weigh each other against their own values and paradigms and come away shaking their respective heads. And, since the small-church people see themselves as the less powerful in the relationship, they cope in ways that reinforce this nonproductive relationship. Ways such as

1. *"You don't care about me."* Small-church people feel left out by the denomination. Overlooked. Not really there. A small-church pastor cried in his (non-alcoholic) beer, "For Pete's sake. The bishop has coffee weekly with the large-church pastors, but he doesn't even have the time to return my phone calls."
2. *"We don't care about you."* We can get along fine without the denomination. What good are they to us anyhow? If it weren't for the mission offering or the apportionment, they wouldn't know we existed. And besides, we don't like their using our dollars to support issues we disagree about. We'd be better off using the money here, you know.
3. *"OK, OK. We'll play your game."* Various ruses are devised to pour the small church into the bureaucratic mold. But the small church is left feeling chagrined and misunderstood.

The mutual misunderstanding and the need to play a different tune—recurrent small church experiences—corroborate the fact that the denomination and the small church are two different social entities. The differences are lived out in the areas of personnel, perspectives, and purpose.

PERSONNEL

One of the great fallacies of current pastoral training is the assumption that the "church universal" means the church generic. Most seminary graduates start out in a small church, from whence an interesting distribution process occurs. Some, ill-suited, drop out of ministry before (hopefully) or after (unfortunately) inflicting much pain on themselves and a small congregation. Some find their calling realized and stay on for many years ministering productively in small church settings. Others pay their dues and move on. Later, you will hear them say, "Small church? Oh, yes. Two of the happiest years of my life were spent in the small church. I know all about it." Or, "Yes, I found a dying small church and five years later I left a growing mid-sized church."

These pastors appear to be successful. They are successful in recognizing that the small church is not for them. So they leave or change the church. But they are ill suited for pastoral ministry in the agrarian sense of the term—in the leading of the flock beside still waters, down the timeworn path between winter and summer pastures, and into the security of the fold at night. These pastors' gifts lie in the areas of planning, "planaging," and envisioning what could yet be. These folk desire "broader" fields of service—at first in a larger church setting, later within the denominational structure. They are after the 99 (while the small-church pastor wastes his or her time chasing after the one). Managing, monitoring, and evaluating are comfortable activities. Their left brains are well developed. They not only know, but they can articulate in clear and reasonable terms, who they are and where they are going. And, mostly, they go to the larger churches and into the bureaucracy.

A good small-church pastor, if offered a denominational position, will say, "Get behind me, Satan." But those in this other group of ministers will only wonder why it took so long to get recognized!

PERSPECTIVE

Any bureaucracy creates its own perspective. Not only are there different people looking at the world, but the world looks different from a ways up the ladder. First of all, it looks like a ladder, feels like a ladder, and tastes like one, too. The cosmology of people on their way up the ladder is *vertical*. The world is something to be climbed and conquered. The small church's cosmology is *horizontal*. Our world is flatter. Oh, sure, it has its share of peaks and valleys, but it is not something to be climbed or even traversed. It is something to be lived in.

A second perspective has to do with time. In the bureaucracy, what is really important is what is going to happen tomorrow. Therefore, planning and preparation are crucial. In the small church, what is really important is what has happened yesterday. Living in light of that gives meaning to life. So, you see, denominational folks believe in the second coming of Christ as their organizing reality, whereas small church folk key in on Christ's first coming, no matter what their verbalized theologies say.

Another perspective has to do with *original sin*. The fundamental sin from which all others flow, from the bureaucracy's point of view, is the tendency of human nature to lapse into patterned behavior (you know, habits, what we did last year at this time) rather than to think everything out. "Being intentional" is tantamount to salvation at denominational headquarters. Whereas, to the small-church person, the idea that by thinking a person can solve the mystery of life—that notion is a basic sin. We should start with the accumulated wisdom of the preceding generations and then make small adjustments from there, if experience requires it.

A fourth difference in perspective has to do with *where heaven is*. One summer my church had a seminarian with us as a pastoral intern. A wonderful, talented, dedicated Christian woman, we could tell she would make a loving pastor once she was ordained in her denomination. And, in order to get ordained, she needed to present her accomplishments during her stay at our church. She was very eager that a Bible study discussion group she initiated continue on into the fall and indefinite future, for then she would have accomplished something and helped to earn herself new credentials. I, too, was eager that this group continue. I hoped it would be a vital part of our life for exactly as long as it was needed, then, whenever it fulfilled itself, in a week or a year, a decade or a generation, I hoped it would die and give its life energy to another form. So we had different perspectives. To me, accomplishments are valuable, but rhythms are more enduring. She was holding up Psalm 90:17: "Let the favor of the Lord our God be upon us, and establish Thou the work of our hands upon us, yea, the work of our hands establish Thou it." I was content with Ecclesiastes 3:2-3: "A time to be born, and a time to die; a time to plant, and a time to pluck up what is planted; a time to kill, and a time to heal; a time to break down, and a time to build up." I knew that one day she would be a good small-church pastor, once she jumped through a few more denominational hoops. At that point, however, heaven meant getting somewhere. For me, heaven is living in harmony with the rhythms and relationships of life.

PURPOSE

I remember a family gathering years ago at which my substantial uncle, in the face of the rest of us unabashedly pigging out, stated most pompously, "I eat to live. I do not live to eat." So, given such permission, we quickly polished off the pie before he could get to it.

But he poses an interesting question. In our lives—in our church lives— what is the means and what is the end? My denomination, which I have experienced as a wonderfully supportive family, occasionally gets a little too enamored of the computer. In the annual report form they send to me, amidst all the budget and attendance numbers requested, they provide a list of 22 activities, such as daycare, drop-in center, and so forth. If your church engages in the activity, the "yes" box is to be checked. If not, the "no" box. Well, once, after 21 "no's," I was not the happiest of campers. It is a discouraging enterprise for a small church to go through. I suspect even a large church comes away wondering how much more do they have to do? And the implicit message is—unintentional as it must be—*doing* is what is important.

You exist to do. Doing is what is valuable to the bureaucracy. I, myself, am not so sure.

In fact, I think it's the other way around. We do to exist. We do what we need to do in order to keep and enhance our life together. Our doing is in the service of our being. Doing is important, but *being* is crucial. Isn't that why the church has always insisted on the preexistence of the Christ? Jesus did not come to exist in the doing of his mission, but from the very nature of his existence flowed the incarnation.

So, too, in Christ's body, Christ's church:

*   From our identity comes our activity
*   From our integrity comes our service
*   From our being comes our doing
*   From our koinonia comes our concern
*   From our internal life comes our external mission

And our being cannot be captured in the listing of our activities, just as one's personality cannot be captured in a photograph, or on one's daily "to do" list.

Someone once said that organizations are what they measure. Unfortunately, for Christ's mission in the small church, the bureaucracy is geared up to measure observable doings. Small-church people tend to register intangibles, such as caring, faithfulness and dependability.

Personnel, perspectives, and purpose are all facets of the difference between a small church as a social system and a national ecclesiastical structure as a social system. Each has its God-given place. Neither is evil or wrong per se. But the mismatch is not acknowledged and appreciated. This must change if small churches are to be liberated for Christ's mission.

The systemic differences between small-church tribal functioning and denominational bureaucratic functioning are manifest in the areas of people, perspective, and purpose. This leaves the bureaucracy able to register one out of four types of small-church mission activity. First, the small church has the ministry of presence in its community; it physically symbolizes God's presence in our midst. Second, the small church conducts an extensive personal ministry. This was evident to me in the days following the death of those young boys and yet so invisible to an outsider. Third, the small church, by living in faith at the margin and emphasizing countercultural values, embodies a pattern of potential redemption for our society as a whole. And, finally, small churches may engage in programmed missions. Unfortunately, this is the only activity that is regularly registered, recognized, and evaluated by transchurch structures. Therefore, gauging faithfulness in small-church mission requires the development of alternative evaluation standards.

Originally published in The Five Stones *(Summer 1999), pp. 13-16; used by permission.*

Chapter 24

RURAL REMNANT:
A METAPHOR OF MISSION
FOR THE RURAL CHURCH

John H. Bennett

In a recent consultation with a northwest Missouri congregation, a penetrating (though not always articulated) question that dominates the life of most small and/or rural congregations put me to the test: "Do you think our congregation has a future?"

Consider this example: The congregation sits in an open-country community (pop. 44), which, like so many northern Missouri communities, represents a demographic nightmare. The 1990 census shows the county population at 8,469, a decline of 27 percent over the last three decades and a shrinkage in the farming population of 44 percent. Within the last decade the community has seen the closing of the elementary school, the grocery store, and the service station. The two institutions remaining in town are a Christian church (Disciples of Christ), with whom I was working, and a United Methodist church, congregations of similar size (that is, worship average of 12 to 15). The congregation enjoys a very good relationship with a female pastor who serves part time and preaches there two Sundays a month (serving another small congregation some 30 miles away on alternate Sundays). Sunday school and a communion service with a lay elder presiding are held on the Sundays of the pastor's absence. To its credit, the congregation maintains a sense of mission, contributing about 15 percent of receipts to outreach causes and has contributed to an independent border ministry in Mexico for the past 25 years.

The questioner was proud of the congregation's history and of its current witness but deeply distressed by the doubtful prospect for its future life and mission. In responding to the question, I took a deep breath, gathered my thoughts, and shared something like this: "The long-term future of this congregation may appear bleak because you are the victim of economic and social forces over which you have no control. The only thing I can tell you about the future is that it's uncertain—and in the care of God. I can also tell you what I've observed: now, you are being the church—preaching, teaching, and sharing at the Table, ministering to each other, and reaching out in mission—you are being a faithful remnant. The challenge before you is to continue to live in the interim between now and whatever the future holds as that faithful remnant. I don't know about the distant future, but I do believe that God has a place for you now and for all the small, rural churches like you, who seek to serve God faithfully in a bigger-is-better culture where rural life is devalued. Your witness is desperately needed; keep the faith here in this place until you are sure that your time has come."

I do not offer this as a model response but, perhaps, as a starting point for reflecting upon a remnant theology in which to ground a strategy for rural ministry and mission. As I drove the four-plus hours home that afternoon, I pondered my response, whether it matched the intensity of the question, and if the kernel of truth it contains might be fleshed out in a more comprehensive reflection and action strategy. What follows is an attempt to start that process.

THEOLOGICAL REFLECTIONS

Remnant Theology

The authors of the Presbyterians' very helpful study of pastoral options for small churches, *New Times—New Call*, contend that larger congregations tend to "live out a theology of abundance and success. . . . a 20th-century cultural expression of kingdom theology" with an emphasis upon growth, successful program, and ministry.[1] The small church, by contrast, "more accurately reflects a theology of the 'faithful remnant.'" The historical setting of the remnant community of the exile differs from that of modern small and/or rural congregations, to be sure. However, there are some factors that contribute to an "exilic" condition for rural communities and congregations:

- their marginalized status, prompting David Ostendorf to declare that "rural America is America's outback"[2]
- the demographic decline in many rural counties and regions

- the predatory forces that prey upon rural communities (for instance, industrialized agriculture, public policy skewed toward corporate agriculture and multinationals, and so forth)
- the perception and, in some cases, the reality of denominational indifference to the needs and interests of rural congregations
- pastors who are not really trained for, nor committed to, a ministry in rural exile

Small and/or rural congregations that claim a vision for ministry in such a context are worthy of the term *faithful remnant* and must be spiritually prepared for the rigors of extended exile.

Marks of the Church

The early church delineated four essential marks of the church which could be found from the moment of its birth (Acts 2:37-47): *kergyma* (proclamation), *didache* (teaching), *koinonia* (community), and *diakonia* (service). To that list I would add a fifth, *oikoumene* (ecumenism), which is inherent in the gospel and in the witness of the church through the ages. It is faithfulness to these marks of the church which determines congregational vitality—not congregational size, not the size of the budget, or any other Madison Avenue measurement. The fundamental questions to be asked are these:

- How is the gospel proclaimed in this congregation? To what extent is this congregation a "good news" place?
- What is the quality of teaching and moral inquiry here?
- What is the evidence that this congregation is a just and compassionate community?
- How is this congregation engaged in servant love in this community and world?
- How does this congregation witness to the unity of the church and the oneness of the human family?

It should be evident that these questions are not size specific and are as challenging and as problematic for the large congregation as for the small/rural one. It is my conviction that few congregations, of any size, are focused on these questions and my further conviction that small/rural congregations are thrown off track of pursuing them because they've been "snookered" by cultural assumptions to believe that the Madison Avenue measurements are the valid ones. They can be disabused of such thoughts by focusing on these fundamental missional questions derived from the historic marks of the church and, thereby, be freed from their feelings of guilt about their smallness and marginalized status. Indeed, they can be led to see that their size and vulnerability are virtues in the realm of God: "But you, O Bethlehem of Ephrathah, who are one of the little clans of Judah, from you shall come forth for me one who is to rule in Israel" (Micah 5:2, NRSV).

THE SPIRITUAL CONTENT OF RURAL LIVING

The Canadian rural sociologist and lay theologian R. Alex Sim, in his book *The Plight of the Rural Church*, has called for "a renewed emphasis on the spiritual content of rural living and a vigorous statement of rural values." Indeed, he warns, "until the rural church takes on a new role as a distinctive rural institution, it will have failed its people, rejected its prophetic mission and ensured its further decline." "The rural church," he notes, "remains all too often a symbol of nostalgia and loss, and is seldom a forerunner and leader in the regeneration of rural society." "But," he says, "the edifice is still there" (that is, a structured spiritual community with the potential for transforming its natural and social environment). That can be accomplished, he contends, by the development of a "rural theology" with two emphases: an environmental focus (relationship with nature) and a renewal of the "social gospel" (relationship with neighbor). Such a theology would empower the rural church "to correct the excesses of urbanization and industrialization" by reaffirming the primary values of "neighborhood and community, caring for one another, sharing resources, smallness and intimacy, transcendence and spirit." Add caring for the earth to this list and we have a broad listing of the rural church's mission agenda.[3]

In summary, the small/rural church is positioned by its size and context to be a vital instrument of God's mission. As David Ray has said with such conviction, "theologically, small churches are the right size to be and do: all that God calls a church to be and to do."[4] The task before us, simply put, is to challenge the small/rural congregations in our care to live up to that call. I suggest that the way for those congregations to live up to that call is by claiming who they are, a rural remnant, empowered by the spirit for faithful witness.

RURAL REMNANT: POTENTIAL MODELS

The Single Congregation

The single congregation can claim its remnant status through a threefold process:

1. biblical and theological reflection upon the "faithful remnant" and upon God's "bias" for smallness
2. serious attention to the historic marks of the church and their implication for the mission of a particular congregation in a particular place
3. use of a reliable methodology for ascertaining congregational and community needs and justice-focused Bible study as a way of encouraging intensive reflection on community mission[5]

Remnant Yokes

The above process can be enhanced when employed in various forms of cooperative ministry:

*   *denominational clusters of congregations* in a county or appropriate geographical area whose ministries are enriched by the networking of the cluster and a process of shared ministries
*   *ecumenical yoked ministry* in a town, or among two or more open-country churches, whose shared life has the added virtue of its witness to the unity of the church
*   *town-and-country yoked ministry* in which a church in the county seat or small town links up with an open-country congregation for mutual support in "blended ministry"
*   *urban-rural linkages in ministry* in which two or more congregations operate in something like a U.S.-Third World "sister congregation" relationship, valuing the vitality of each congregation, sharing in various ministries, and forming solidarity around mutual social and economic concerns

These, or other strategies of mission, need to be employed by small/rural congregations as they live out their calling as faithful remnants of God's people and claim a hopeful future.

Remnant Leadership

It is evident that the predominant form of pastoral leadership for the rural church will be that of licensed, commissioned, or bivocational clergy. Small and rural churches have been "priced out of the market" of the full-time, seminary-trained model of pastoral leadership, although many still cling to this model with a wistful yearning. Some yoked ministries are still able to support a full-time person but they are increasingly rare and are often fraught with the tension of a leadership style that is out of harmony with the congregational setting or that bears conflicting expectations. A fully trained lay ministry can provide a creative alternative to such dysfunctional relationships and empower the congregation in its ministry. Perhaps, in the 21st century, we shall see the Reformation principle of the "priesthood of all believers" fully appropriated by the church. The rural church may lead the way!

I close these reflections by sharing Alex Sims's reflections on the parable of the mustard seed:

After buying a farm in the Ottawa Valley, we decided to plow a meadow long used as a pasture. There was no sign of mustard, but once the field was cultivated and the land brought into good tilth, we were surprised to find the mustard plant with its brilliant yellow flower competing sturdily with a crop of oats. Apparently, the seed had lain dormant all those years in the patient earth awaiting friendly circumstances to permit it to germinate and spring back to life and reproduction. Rural Canada (and rural America) awaits just such a spiritual awakening.

Notes

1. *New Times—New Call: A Manual of Pastoral Options for Small Churches* (Louisville: Evangelism and Church Development, PCUSA, 1991)

2. David Ostendorf, executive director, Center for New Community, Chicago (address at McCormick Theological Seminary, Chicago, 1986).

3. R. Alex Sim, *The Plight of the Rural Church* (Toronto: United Church Publishers, 1990).

4. David Ray, *The Big Small Church Book* (Cleveland: The Pilgrim Press, 1992).

5. Such as the "Renewing Rural Iowa" survey developed by Prairie Fire Rural Action, Des Moines, Iowa and upon which our Renewing Rural Missouri program is patterned, or the Rural Social Science Education materials developed by Texas

A&M as a resource for group study of rural demographics and the dynamics of rural communities and congregations.

Originally published in the Small Church Newsletter *(Missouri School of Religion Center for Rural Ministry; Sept. 1996) and reprinted in* The Five Stones *(Summer 1999), pp. 2-5; used by permission.*

Chapter 25

ECUMENICAL SHARED MINISTRY: LAST RESORT OR GOD'S WILL?

David Ray

During the 17th-century Reformation struggle for religious freedom in Great Britain, Puritan Richard Baxter wrote: "In essentials, unity; in non-essentials, liberty; in all things, charity." Numberless struggling churches of every stripe resist encouragement toward unity or cooperation, struggle to hang on to their liberty or autonomy, and are suspicious of anything smacking of charity or sharing. Willingness to consider some form of cooperative ministry is often resisted until all other options are exhausted. What an amazing grace it would be if the economic crisis confronting these churches led them beyond mere survival to unity transcending their liberty and charity in all things via some form of ecumenical sharing.

The way things are is not necessarily the way things have to be or ought to be. The way things are is that most churches would rather be independent and have "our own pastor." Many churches that can no longer maintain their independence would opt for association with a church of their own denomination rather than one of a different tradition. As one who is a small-church pastor, denominational area minister, and self-confessed "ecumaniac," I see the various forms of ecumenical shared ministry less as last resorts and more as reemerging models of what God might be seeking to create.

The biblical, historical, and theological mandate is clear. Paul wrote to the Roman church: "For as in one body we have many members, and not all the members have the same function, so we, who are many, are one body in Christ, and individually we are members of one another." St. Ignatius wrote to a second-century church: "Do everything in common; Unite in one prayer, one petition, one mind, one hope, in love and faultless joy. . . . So make haste, all of you, to come together as to one temple of God, around one altar, around the one Jesus Christ." And Karl Barth unequivocally asserts in his *Church Dogmatics* (vol. 4, 1: 675):

> There is no justification, theological, spiritual, or biblical, for the existence of a plurality of Churches genuinely separated in this way and mutually excluding one another internally and therefore externally. A *plurality* of churches . . . means a plurality of *lords.* . . . There may be good grounds for the rise of these divisions. There may be serious obstacles to their removal. There may be many things which can be said by way of interpretation and mitigation. But this does not alter the fact that every division as such is a deep riddle, a *scandal.*

Denominational separatism and local church independence seem contrary to important themes in our biblical, historical, and theological tradition.

Churches (especially small ones) resist combining forces with other churches for the same reasons that families resist losing family identity: They feel like family. They have their own way of doing things. They have their own history and traditions. They fear loss of power and influence. They lack models that illustrate how the various forms of sharing might look and feel. Organizational independence is simpler than creating and maintaining a shared arrangement. As a result, there is no attractive vision of what a future shared ministry and mission might be like.

Denominational bodies have actively or benignly avoided ecumenical sharing ventures, except when church closure is the only alternative. They've done this for the very same reasons that local churches have been hesitant or resistant. They've preferred to facilitate some form of sharing between churches of their own denomination. What seems to be in the denomination's best interest needs to be weighed against what's in the best interest of the local church and its local community. The faithful witness and effectiveness of a unifying body of Christ in a community ought to take precedence over denominational efficiency and purity.

ADVANTAGES AND DISADVANTAGES

There are several reasons why some form of shared ministry may provide the most effective and faithful way of maintaining and expanding Christian ministry and mission in many locales. I see these options as particularly advantageous in the upper-midwest and plains states where rural populations are declining and communities tend to be farther apart. The *advantages* are:

1. Some form of ecumenical shared ministry is consistent with biblical, historical, and theological visions of the church.
2. By its witness and combined influence, an ecumenical shared ministry can help move a community to greater commonality and cooperation.
3. In the same way that each partner in a marriage brings a reservoir of history, tradition, and understandings to share with the other for the benefit of both, the same is true of churches of different denominational backgrounds that join forces. Rather than denying or forgetting their particular backgrounds, each should prize, draw on, and share their heritage.
4. Two or more churches can combine strengths and resources for mutual benefit and greater effectiveness.
5. Where there are limited financial, organizational, and human resources, some form of sharing can compensate for the difficulties and limitations with which each separate church struggles. In particular, a sharing between churches can mean they can afford better, more effective pastoral leadership.
6. Churches of differing denominational connections ought to be able to call on the resources of each denomination to strengthen their shared ministry and mission. And there is the potential of contributing to the strengthening of each denomination.

While the benefits are several and significant, there are *potential dangers and problems:*

1. If the sharing is seen as only a marriage of necessity rather than a new opportunity, the participating churches may be satisfied with just getting by and surviving.
2. If the partnering has been a "force fit" rather than a marriage of compatibility, the relationship may remain or grow cool, distant, or hostile.

3. It's more difficult to find able pastors to serve shared ministries. The result can be an ineffectual or merely maintenance ministry and a short pastoral tenure.
4. If the shared ministry has one pastor serving two or more churches, it can often feel like a bigamous relationship, with all the difficult dynamics that go with multiple spouses.
5. In a culture where the standard for a "real" church has been and is one pastor serving one independent church on a full-time basis, a shared ministry can feel second class or quasi-legitimate to pastor and churches, resulting in serious self-esteem issues.
6. Unless both denominations and churches are sensitive and understanding, an ecumenical shared ministry can result in the churches feeling like they are serving and pacifying two masters.

There are four primary categories of shared ministries, with many variations. A *yoke* is when two or more churches share a pastor or pastors and perhaps some programming, while maintaining their separate identities and most of their autonomy. A *federation* is when two or more churches join forces to share pastoral leadership, building, and programming, while maintaining separate allegiances. A *larger* or *cooperative parish* is when three or more churches share more than one staff, programming, and resources. A *merged church* is when two or more churches consolidate their membership, organization, and resources to form one new church. Which of these options is the appropriate or feasible option depends on the context, personalities, and other particularities of the situation. Only a wise and sensitive helper can assist churches to seek, find, and implement the shared ministry that is most conducive to their well being.

PRINCIPLES

Creating and sustaining a shared ministry is more art than science. Yet there is accumulated wisdom and principles that can help avoid some of the landmines and pitfalls. Some of these principles are:

1. The potential partners must be compatible. Compatibility is determined by a combination of denominational background, understanding of "church," church size, congregational self-image, organizational style,

world view, and role in the community. It is also determined by intangibles. When the leaders and members are brought together, watch to determine whether they like each other, get along, and have important things in common. If there's commonality, a shared ministry may work; if there isn't, it won't.

2. The local churches' denominational leadership should be involved throughout the process. They have accumulated wisdom, leadership skills, and resources that are crucial to the success of the sharing.

3. A shared ministry should be customized, not mass produced. It needs to accommodate all the variations and nuances of the situation. Customization takes longer to create, but has much better potential for succeeding.

4. Use planning methods that are careful, creative, and collegial. As much as possible make decisions by consensus, not majority rule.

5. Seek, develop, and flesh out a shared, common, and faithful vision that is more than mere survival. Sing the old hymns and learn new ones. Do creative Bible study and preach pregnant scriptures. Get people praying carefully and expectantly.

6. All the people of both or all the churches need to be included and involved throughout the process. Listen to their fears, work through their anger, honor their ideas, channel their energy, involve them in the new creation. This takes longer and can be "messy." But if people aren't brought along, they will be lost along the way.

7. Find elements in their individual traditions and identities that can be appropriated and built upon. Find compatibility and connections in their histories. Keep and use their holy objects. As is done in weddings, find ways to symbolize and ritualize the joining together of separate entities.

8. Tune and test-drive the customized shared ministry before sending it out on its own for the long haul.

***

Several years ago I was preaching in a Baptist church in Rwanda. Using the apostle Paul's image of the Body of Christ with its many interdependent organs, I tried to help my hearers visualize and identify with the wider church about which they knew little. At the end of the sermon, I invited the congregation to participate in the ancient Christian custom of passing the peace of Christ. Unfortunately, the missionary translator in translating from my English to their Rwandan language used the word *piece* instead of *peace*. There was much confusion and consternation as people considered how they would pass a *piece* of Christ!

For much too long and far too often we have lived with and perpetuated a Body of Christ in pieces, rather than seeking to build a deep and lasting peace within the Body of Christ. Customized versions of ecumenical shared ministries can help us move from a church in pieces to a peace-filled church.

Originally published in The Five Stones *(Summer 1994), pp. 13-15; used by permission.*

Chapter 26

BECOMING A 30-MILE CHURCH

Gary E. Farley

He certainly didn't set out to do so. He probably didn't intend to do so. It may have been more a consequence of change than a cause. However, community boundaries in rural America have been redrawn. For better or for worse, the "Wal-Mart town" has become the dominant community across the landscapes. Sam Walton's success story of planting nearly 2,000 discount stores, mostly in rural places, has certainly altered community patterns. And since churches relate to communities, church life too will be different.

THE 30-MILE RURAL CHURCH

The basic fact is that the old six-mile communities in which America was settled and churched in the 19th century are being replaced with 30-mile communities. When Wal-Mart comes to town, other chains and franchises follow. Retail trade shifts from the crossroads village and hamlets to the Wal-Mart town. Typically, this town draws consumers from about 15 miles in each direction. As it does, the economic function of the villages within 15 miles of the Wal-Mart town dries up. Often schools are consolidated into the Wal-Mart town as are other services. Many times a sense of psychic depression grips the village as its stores and school are boarded up.

From the perspective of rural sociology, the eight to 15 villages that lie within expanded trade and service areas of the emerging Wal-Mart town are becoming like neighborhoods with a city. That is, people live in these villages and around them, but they work and shop and have most of their needs met in the Wal-Mart town. If you will look at a map, let me give you an example. Take Johnson County, Missouri. Scattered across it are the villages of Pittsville, Columbus, Fayetteville, Valley City, Kingsville, Centerview, Montserrat, Knobnoster, Latour, Quick City, Medford, Chilhowee, Holden, Post Oak and Leeton. Near the center is Warrensburg. Most of the villages are along railroad lines. Before 1950, most of them had stores, a school, a bank, a church or churches, a physician or two, and a grain elevator. Today, most of these institutions, other than the churches, have been consolidated and expanded in Warrensburg. So, most of the villages have become, in effect, low-density neighborhoods of Warrensburg or Johnson County. This same pattern is repeated again and again across rural America.

In most instances, far fewer people live in and around these villages than did in 1950. And many of those who do live in these towns nevertheless spend much of their time away from the village. Whereas a village like Chilhowee or Kingsville once played a primary role in the life of its citizens, it has been reduced to a secondary or a tertiary role. Will the village and rural church follow the lead of businesses and the professions? Will these churches die and be replaced by churches in the Wal-Mart town? Perhaps some, but not necessarily for all.

Logic would seem to suggest that the prospects for village and open-country churches in places losing function and population is not good. Most of these congregations see themselves serving a "church field" that extends about three miles in each direction. And this field is in decline. Adding to their woes, frequently, is the fact that one or more of the churches in the Wal-Mart town is aggressively becoming a "full-service," 30-mile church. It offers programs and activities for children, youth, young families, and seniors. It has fine facilities (including, perhaps, a family-life center). It has a staff of well-trained specialists. Its demands on most members are limited. Like a "religious" Wal-Mart, it offers what most folk want at a price they can afford. Often the village pastor sees car after car of well-scrubbed families drive the 6, 12, or 15 miles past his or her little church to the big church in the Wal-Mart town. In visiting these families, they tell the pastor, "We like your church, but the programs at the big church meet our needs better." What is the little church to do?

Three Basic Principles

I believe that Sam Walton's autobiography offers some principles for the churches outside the emerging Wal-Mart town may find applicable. First, *resist the temptation to take on the big Wal-Mart town church head-to-head.* The village or country church cannot do what the large church can do any more than a small hardware store, clothing shop, or dry goods store can compete directly with Wal-Mart.

Second, *find a niche.* Walton, for example, advises the local hardware store to focus on service; that is, to train clerks to help homeowners understand how to do a repair job and what they need to complete the job. His idea is that the smaller store can find a need that the mass merchandiser is unable to meet and supply it. I see some village and open-country churches doing just this. One has become the "country-and-western" option for folk in a large Wal-Mart town. Trail ride ministries at rodeos and a gospel string band are among its activities. It draws people from all around who want to ride horses, make music, and be around rodeos. It will never become a large church, but it's a very healthy one. It is reaching people that the big-town church cannot. People drive past the full-service church on the way to this distinctive congregation.

Another rural church found itself gifted with persons with drama skills. It decided to produce a passion play during Easter Week. And, although it is far from the Wal-Mart town, people came. In fact, thousands attend annually. This church found a niche and created an identity for itself. It performs a ministry.

Still another rural church hit on the idea of ministering to "home-schooler" families. The pastor and his wife recognized that home-schooled children need to find ways to socialize with other children, while their parents need a support group. So they networked the home-schooling families and invited them to their church on a weekday afternoon for a time when the children could play together while the parents shared resources and techniques. In time, several of these families became a part of their church.

Other examples abound. All across the country, village and open-country churches have realized that their ministry to a six-mile place was not working and that they could not compete with the big, full-service church. So, they found a niche and applied the third principle from Sam Walton— *they extended their field.* They became a 30-mile church. That is, they actively sought to reach all those within the new 30-mile Wal-Mart town community (in which their old six-mile field was a neighborhood) who needed a particular service or who wished to provide a specific ministry. For many village and open-country churches this seems to be their best hope for the future.

NINE KEYS TO THE NEW RURAL COMMUNITY

So how does a church go about becoming a 30-mile, niche-oriented congregation? Here again Sam Walton's autobiography may offer some clues.

1. *The Need to Change*. Sam Walton recognized that he needed to change the way he did business. He saw that his small variety store on the courthouse square in rural America was doomed, for it could not compete in its current place and mode with the discounters. This is true for many rural churches.

2. *Listening*. Walton listened to his customers, to those he wanted for customers, to his employees, and to his competitors. He saw an opportunity to become the leading discounter in the small towns in the Midwest. He learned how to do it and pursued it with total commitment, continually learning. Listening and learning will need to be important characteristics of a village church that decides to become a 30-mile niche church. Crucial, of course, will be finding a niche for the church to serve. You discover this by asking questions and by listening to find out the church's needs, expectations, goals, hopes, and comfort zone. If you listen long and well you will discover a ministry that can be the new "stackpole" for your church.

3. *Think Small*. Walton said that he never abandoned thinking like a small-town independent merchant. He wanted to be ever-sensitive to the expectations of his customers. He made them number one. For him, success was measured in value given. Of course, being a church member is a much deeper relationship than buying a shopping cart full of clothing, tools, and toys at a Wal-Mart. The sense of caring and being cared for is an important need for church members. Being "like family" is a quality that must be guarded.

4. *Involve the People.* Encourage each member to share the vision of the mission. In the quest to be a 30-mile church, also take care of the "front-line" troops who are networking out across the area talking up the church, inviting, sharing their witness. See every role as vital. Reward and encourage people. As new folk are reached, seek to grow them from being consumers of ministry to being providers. Care for families. Don't allow the quest to find your niche result in your members feeling neglected.

5. *Be Enthusiastic.* When a little village church measures itself by a big Wal-Mart church and when it compares the decline of its six-mile community with the growth of the Wal-Mart town, it is subject to depression. But if it can find, for instance, a food ministry that God blesses, then it can feel good about itself. The pastor needs to call attention to the victories being won through this ministry. Praise God for all these blessings. The worship should be a time of praise and inspiration. The church must come to recognize that it has an important role in God's plan for that 30-mile community.

6. *Constantly Monitor What You Are Doing.* Walton conducted a weekly Saturday morning meeting of his management team. They shared what they were seeing, sensing, hearing, and doing. This made it possible for everyone to know where the corporation was going and problems could be nipped in the bud. Church council and deacon meetings can have a similar role in a church. Communication cannot be left to chance.

7. *Take Risks.* Walton shared how he tried many different things and encouraged his managers to try things provided they were germane to the basic missions of the corporation. To move from being a stable six-mile village or open-country church doing all the things churches are supposed to do, to being a 30-mile church focused on a unique ministry will involve risk. Folks will say, "But we never did it this way before." True. However, if you can demonstrate that this is only a new means to time-honored biblically based functions, many, if not most, will proceed in concert with you. Most of these churches long to recapture the excitement of "the glory years." What you are proposing is that this be accomplished in ways appropriate to the current context. It is a matter of finding, defining, selling, inspiring, equipping, and leading in the accomplishment of the work God has for this church in this time.

8. *Be a Part of the New 30-Mile Community.* Early on, Wal-Mart was criticized for taking from and contributing little to the community. This seems to have struck a responsive note in Sam Walton. He goes to great pains in his autobiography to rebut this criticism. The application to churches is obvious. As we move from being a church for a little six-mile community, perhaps the church will need to refocus upon the concerns, events, and needs of the larger 30-mile community. Here it will be only one of several churches. Cooperation will be called for. For example, within the Southern Baptist family cooperative events can be sponsored by the association. Several associations are now working with old six-mile churches to identify a 30-mile ministry, equip the church to do that ministry, provide support from sister congregations, and applaud victories. The associational vision is that of a family of churches addressing various people groups, lifestyle groups, and ministry needs. It seeks to make the slogan, "A Church for Everyone," a reality. The association will no longer seek to have 27 or more congregations with 50 or more ministries targeting almost any group within its bounds.

Intentionally or not, Sam Walton was the creator, explorer, and mapper of the new 30-mile rural community. He achieved great success there. His observations seem to be applicable to church life. I have shared my thinking about this. I encourage you to do the same. I hope that many of you will seek to lead your six-mile rural church to become a 30-mile church. I hope that you can get your association to be an active player in this.

9. *Support One Another.* Finally, a note to the full-service, Wal-Mart-town pastors. Most of what Sam Walton discovered is applicable to your church as well, with one difference: While doing your best to be the Wal-Mart type church, gently encourage the older six-mile churches to find a niche. Point out some ministries that they can do that you cannot. Follow God's calling to be almost as concerned about the health and well-being of the other churches as you are of your own. God has given to your church the awesome responsibility of leadership. In all likelihood God's plan is not for only one church within that 30-mile community, but many different churches. As the lead church, you can enable this to happen.

Originally published in The Five Stones *(Fall 1995), pp. 2-5; used by permission.*

Chapter 27
ORGANIZING FOR MISSION AND MINISTRY IN KENTUCKY'S RURAL CHURCHES

Bennett D. Poage

John and Sally are in their middle 50s and have been tobacco farmers since they took over John's father's farm 35 years ago. They are third-generation members of the Wide View Christian Church in rural Kentucky. John has been an elder for 20 years and Sally is active in the Christian Women's Fellowship (CWF). Two of their three children are married and they are the proud grandparents of a grandson and two granddaughters. The married children work off the farm but live close by. Their youngest son, now 21, lives at home and works with his father on the farm. Both he and his father anticipate that he is the "heir apparent" for the ancestral land. Farming the land, growing the crop, and keeping the cattle has been a hard life, but one full of rewards: a sense of place, a closeness with creation, the fulfillment of planting and harvest. By and large it has provided a comfortable living.

Church has been a vital part of this life. The children were taught about God's world here and baptized in the faith. But for the past two decades more and more young people have moved away and the "mainstays" of the congregation keep dying with fewer and fewer to take their place. The church has passed from stability to decline.

In years past the church had more impact in the community and more outreach beyond its own needs. The men's class sponsored link missionaries. The CWF sent blankets to the victims of poverty and catastrophic events worldwide and sponsored needy children in Asia and Africa. The youth collected soup labels to buy school equipment for an Indian reservation. And when disasters struck in the community—families burned out, sudden deaths, or accidents—the congregation made tables groan with covered dishes, money mysteriously appeared to meet needs, and crops were planted or harvested as the need might be.

These days there are not enough men left to sponsor missions, and perpetual Bible study and canned lessons are punctuated with talk about the need for a new church roof and the growing wave of public animosity toward tobacco: new federal taxes, lower quotas, more imports, more health restrictions. The go-to-church clothes are older, so are the cars driven to church, so are the faces staring dismally at a darkening and troubled future. The CWF meets faithfully every month for the lesson and lunch but there is not enough energy or money to reach beyond the needs of the local congregation. Survival is a powerful instinct for social institutions as well as people. The women now talk of families who have had to sell their farms and move away, of the increasing number of unchurched families in the community, of run-down homes and communities, of the growing food-stamp line at the Department for Human Resources. They talk in discouraged and worried tones and hope is rarely mentioned.

The youth group hasn't existed for almost 10 years. The few young people left are becoming increasingly busy with school activities. The congregation misses young laughter, buoyant spirits, hope and optimism, the freshness and idealism of youth.

A gray, stale wind is blowing at Wide View and the talk is about reliving the past, about keeping things the way they are, about paying the preacher, while minimizing the heating and the electric bills. Now when farmers in the community and even in the congregation face economic disaster, no dishes are carried in, no money is collected, no help is ever offered. Men and women talk in whispers of bad management, over-extended credit, too much spending, too many trips to town. The victim becomes the object of blame. The circle of wagons at the Wide View camp are driven tighter and frightened and angry faces look out with no compassion or understanding.

How can we talk of mission and ministry when we are barely surviving? How can we consider outreach when we need a new roof? How can we relate to community needs when we are so unsure of our own well-being? Let's just sing the old familiar songs, repeat the old words, and hire a minister who will give us comfort and peace of mind.

THE NATURE OF THE RURAL CHURCH

Unfortunately, a growing number of rural churches are assuming the characteristics of the Wide View congregation. Because of shrinking farm income in Kentucky, exacerbated in the last few years by declining tobacco quotas, a deadly domino effect has been set in motion: "(1) a deterioration in the quality of church staff via lower salaries; (2) a general inability to obtain staff and to maintain the physical facility; (3) a likely shift to less-educated ministers, typically obtained from the 'independent' wing of the Christian Church; (4) a shift to more conservative 'survival' programming at a time when the congregation should be reaching out to community needs the most; (5) a general congregational retrenchment process that becomes a cumulative process of stagnation and eventual decay—a lingering death. Such a process will ultimately contribute to the death of the community as well as to the death of the congregation."[1]

This growing entrenchment in Kentucky's tobacco churches is supported by many of the traditional characteristics attributed to all small rural churches. These characteristics include:

- An oral "insider" tradition
- A "single cell," or family-like social organization
- An informal leadership structure

Change comes slowly, if at all, for these family-like congregations. However, some change may occur through *community trends*: the aging of the congregation, a shift from rural to urban, and so forth. Change, of course, may be legislated (but it rarely is). *Legislated change* (frequently coerced) may mean, at worst, a split in the congregation or a reduction in giving. At best, it may mean a reversal of the vote the following Sunday. The gentlest form of change is *friendly persuasion*, but this typically comes only from the inside or from outsiders who have gained a high level of trust. This level of trust comes from a consistent, positive, and nonthreatening presence. Closely related to this type of change is *planned alternatives*. In a true family-like congregation, this is rarely done. But with a trusted consultant, long-range planning can take place, especially if it comes out of serious long-term needs related to survival.

Nonpositive forms of change include *no option left*, which is a bit like legislated or coerced change. It's tricky, can backfire in unforeseen ways, and feelings almost always end up being hurt. A second negative form is *major paradigm shifts*, the building burns down or the bottom falls out of the tobacco market. In this form, change is really not being effected, only the consequences are being dealt with. The results may be very positive or very negative, depending on the leadership executed during this tricky period.

In all change, a process occurs akin to grief, that is, the loss of a loved one, a shift in economic fortune, retirement, or a major church program change. According to Larry Brown, "Stages include:

- Shock and numbness
- Searching and yearning
- Disorientation and disorganization
- Resolution and reorganization

Anger, fear, and hurt must be dealt with in all these stages in order to finally get to stage four." [2]

MISSION AND MINISTRY GROUNDINGS

When faced with such shifting economic and cultural paradigms rural congregational leaders frequently feel bewildered and insignificant. Given the massive needs on one hand, and dwindling resources on the other, how can they rise to the challenge of being faithful to God's mission in their community?

The answer may lie in being audacious enough to take the first step, in not allowing the enormity of the task to immobilize the effort, or in taking God's great commission seriously enough to do something about it. Part of the answer also relates to the support, encouragement, and engagement of the "whole church." The "larger church" must not allow rural congregations to become frozen in their response. They need leadership, prayer, and financial support.

John Bennett, director of the Missouri School of Religion Center of Rural Ministry, in an article for *The Disciple* magazine says, "The mission challenge is a significant one because rural America remains in crisis."[3] Bennett goes on to quote David Ostendorf, rural/urban ministry consultant and a former director of Prairie Fire Rural Action, Des Moines, Iowa, who

. . . calls for a mission response which is keyed to the rural
reality and focused on the renewal of rural communities and
congregations through the engagement of congregations in community mission.

Key elements of that response will include: 1) rural clergy preparation and training which includes an emphasis on rural socio-eco-
nomics and the dynamics of rural communities and congregations;
2) faith formation and leader development for rural laity focused
on empowering laity for their ministry in the world; 3) developing a
strategy for evangelism that is centered in community mission; 4)
rural issues networking and advocacy with allied agencies, institutions and organizations; 5) cooperative parish development, the
"yoking" of congregations denominationally or ecumenically for
the enhancement of ministry and mission; 6) global mission education which affirms and interprets the global connections among
the world's rural peoples.[4]

Too often rural congregations (and *many* urban congregations) view
mission as something extra to do after "we take care of all the internal
needs of our congregation." It's seen as frosting on the cake, not as the
cake itself. Scripture, however, teaches that the church exists *by* mission,
not *for* mission, as fire exists by burning. That mission is following a God
already at work. As Acts 1:8 indicates, mission is not a duty, or something
nice to do, but a spontaneous act of faith.

MODELS OF HOPE

This is the mission context that the rural church must operate in as it considers the way(s) it will be engaged in mission and ministry. As the planning
process takes place, six critical leadership and organizational needs must be
engaged. All models of mission and ministry must address each of these
needs to be ultimately successful. They are: (1) *the need for vision*; (2)
the need for structure; (3) *the need for early success*; (4) *the need for
continuity*; (5) *the need for praise*; and (6) *the need for growth*. These
apply both to the ministries of individual congregations and of cooperative
parishes.

1. *The need for vision* starts with a well-designed, long-range planning process. After the general concepts for mission and ministry have been accepted by the congregation or the church board, a steering or planning committee needs to be put in place. It should be inclusive of gender and of age groups in the congregation. The purpose of this committee is to educate itself about mission and ministry and to involve, educate, and motivate as many individual members of the congregation(s) as possible. It is important for the committee and the congregation to be informed about what is possible and to be empowered to accomplish that possibility. This involvement is frequently accomplished through an "every-member survey" or "inventory." This survey or inventory is a way to find out what the congregation wants to do for themselves and how they want to be involved in mission with the community. This process may take six months to one year. *Don't rush it.* It's critical that a program of ministry and mission not be implemented until the planning process is complete. Chris Hobgood, Disciples Regional Minister in the Capital Area and past Executive Minister of the Christian Church in Arkansas, says, "I am convinced that the primary step to the effectiveness of ministry in the small congregation is developing lay leaders who, individually, have a vision broader than that which has driven the congregation in the past."[5]

United Methodist Cooperative Parish Development Specialists say that 20 percent of any given congregation want to do more ministry and mission than the other 80 percent is willing to do. This committee of vision, congregationally or in relation to a cooperative parish, attracts that 20 percent.

2. *The need for structure* is common for both cooperative parishes and individual congregations. Once the steering or planning committee has completed its work, some level of structuring needs to take place. This can range from formal nonprofit incorporation (with charter and by-laws), in the case of the cooperative parish, to permanent committee status in the case of individual congregations. In either case, the organization must grow from a well-thought-out and well-conceived purpose statement (in cooperative parishes this is included in the charter). The purpose statement comes from an assessment of need, for example, from answers given in an every-member survey.

In addition to the purpose statement, structure must include: (1) a systematic way to elect committee members that is inclusive of gender and age groupings in the congregation; (2) a way to elect officers, then establish terms of office and job descriptions; (3) necessary subcommittees, both standing and temporary, with the authority of the committees spelled out; and (4) a way to communicate with the rest of the congregation (that is, sharing reports, receiving requests, and making recommendations).

Carl S. Dudley, in *Basic Steps toward Community Ministry* says four aspects of good organizational management are the most difficult: "(a) How will you fit the social ministry into the existing congregational management style? (b) How will you hold a common vision, yet accomplish each step along the way? (c) How will you expand your base without losing your constituency? (d) How will your ministry empower the people you are trying to serve?"[6] These questions need to be fully considered as the organizational structure is developed.

3. *The need for early success* is a principle of good community organizing. If all of the objectives or needs to be met are difficult, hence tending to be long range, the committee or cooperative parish will become discouraged and lose interest.

Short-term objectives will undoubtedly appear from an every-member survey. Better organization to meet direct service needs in the community, for example, can give early success. On the other hand, meeting developmental needs takes longer, and organizing for advocacy usually falls into the long-range category. Nonetheless, some developmental needs, such as organizing for literacy and general high school equivalency (GED) education, can be met relatively soon. In the Garrard County Cooperative Parish,[7] for example, literacy/GED classes were organized within the first year. Early on, these classes produced a feeling of great success among the co-op member congregations. If the need to be met is truly great in the community, as was the need for literacy/GED in Garrard County, small efforts to engage the need will meet with overwhelming community participation and hence success.

4. *The need for continuity* is paramount in programs of mission and ministry. No program which starts and ends with each successive minister can be effective. For that reason, and since the longevity of ministers tends to be short in most rural churches, the leadership of mission committees and/or cooperative parishes must be lay persons. Chris Hobgood says, "We in ministry would be wise not to barge in with big interventions

in small congregations; rather, equip lay leaders to make these moves. After all, they, too, are ministers. And their word is what is heard in the small, lay-led congregations."[8]

This does not mean the licensed or ordained minister has no place in mission leadership; quite the contrary. The professional minister can have voice without vote in meetings, but, more importantly, the professional minister can, and should, become staff for implementing the program. If judicatory ministers are involved they should also become staff of the program. But in all cases, lay people should lead the committee and/or the cooperative parish. (Admittedly, there may be situations where exceptions have to be made, but this should always be done with the full knowledge that continuity and lay ownership are being compromised.)

5. *The need for praise* is often overlooked when organizing a missions program or a cooperative parish. Nonetheless, nothing builds confidence, pride, and ownership like praise. In both the Garrard County Cooperative Parish (GCCP) and in the Raccoon John Smith Cooperation,[9] organizers have been very deliberate in setting up opportunities for praise. Praise comes naturally when the stories of origin, struggle, and success are told in formal and informal settings. The GCCP lay leaders, for example, have become accomplished teachers in how to organize and run a cooperative parish. They are involved several times each year in teaching seminarians (enrolled in Appalachian Ministries Educational Resource Center Educational Programs) and others about the parish. A trip to the Disciples General Assembly in Indianapolis to give a cooking demonstration and to sell cookbooks is now a part of the cooperative folk tradition. It is told and retold with great relish and appreciation. The Raccoon John Smith Cooperation, primarily focused around their annual meeting events—such as actors playing Raccoon John Smith or Alexander Campbell (early leaders in the Disciple Church)—has had similar experiences of sharing with, and being praised by, the community and the larger church.

6. *The need for growth* is last, but nonetheless critical, in the litany of needs for a successful mission and ministry effort. Someone has said that organizations or organized efforts can never stand still. They have to grow or they begin to die.

An important aspect in growth is the need to build in points of evaluation in the organization's life. Evaluations should be done annually, as a part of the annual report preparation. Also, a major program evaluation should be built into the organization's life every three to five years. This evaluation should give an objective look at accomplishments, weak and strong areas, and point to opportunities for growth.

Recently, an informal evaluation of the Garrard County Cooperative Parish program disclosed the need to grow in areas of advocacy for tobacco farmers and in addressing the need for a countywide ecumenical Habitat For Humanity program. Likewise, an informal evaluation of the Raccoon John Smith Cooperation, precipitated by a change in leadership, pointed to a need for growth in the area of education and advocacy for migrant farm workers in the cooperation's area.

Advocacy—using our power as citizens and "people of faith" to shape government policy—is the toughest area of mission and ministry growth in the rural congregation or cooperative parish, but one of the most needed areas. Moreover, advocacy is the logical culmination of growth for ministries that have started with, and continue to address, direct service and developmental needs. Advocacy rounds out or completes a full mission and ministry program.

A manual from National Impact speaks out for the need for advocacy in this way: "Advocacy has a special meaning among religious people. It means speaking up for the poor and injured—powerless people who are intentionally or unintentionally hurt by the actions of others. But advocacy also means speaking up for our values, human society and the future. When others have justice and know peace, we are more secure. And when we do our part for others, we are spiritually enriched."[10]

Nonetheless, advocacy is typically controversial in the rural congregation. In 30 surveys completed by lay and clergy persons from rural churches in east-central Kentucky, about half believed that clergy should preach on rural justice themes and the other half believed they should preach strictly from the Bible. These respondents seemed to suggest that the Bible has nothing to say on matters of justice.

It seems that a lot of scripturally inspired teaching must be done before advocacy can be accepted by everyone as a legitimate ministry of the rural congregation or parish. Nonetheless, at their best congregations should, as Lorette Picciano-Honson, Executive Director of the Rural Coalition, stated,

> . . . stand with the people; hear what they say; and collect them together to create alternate vision, try out models, propose

Inside the Small Church

policies, build networks and renew hope. After all, most policy change occurs because someone has the audacity to make it happen. Social, economic and environmental justice are simply not priorities of the agribusiness and other interests which have been most aggressive and influential in constructing our current policies. Our experience of the last decade demonstrates that most of all, we need the audacity to believe that God is with each of us and together we have the ability to understand, to act and to make policy which manifests justice instead of injustice.[11]

As John and Sally face the future in their rural Kentucky church they have the choice of doing old, familiar, and comfortable things, thereby ignoring the community, its issues, and its needs. They can be safe and avoid the demands of the cross, "Whoever does not carry the cross and follow me cannot be my disciple" (Luke 14:27). Or they can choose to pick up the cross of mission and ministry in Christ's name and become his disciples in their own congregation and community. The choice is theirs *and* it is ours.

NOTES

1. Bennett D. Poage, *The Tobacco Church: A Manual For Congregational Leaders* (Richmond, Ky.: The Christian Church [Disciples of Christ] in Kentucky, 1993), p. 85.
2. Larry Brown, Small Church Conference Workshop on "How to Affect Change," Jefferson City, Mo., Missouri School of Religion, July 1987.
3. John Bennett, "Insignificant You Are Not," *The Disciple* (February 1994), p. 6.
4. Bennett, "Insignificant You Are Not," pp. 6-7.
5. William Chris Hobgood, "Where There Is No Vision," *The Small Church Newsletter* (June 1994), p. 4.
6. Carl S. Dudley, *Basic Steps toward Community Ministry* (Bethesda, Md.: The Alban Institute, 1992), p. 80.
7. Incorporated in 1987, the Garrard County Cooperative Parish is supported and directed by three small-to-midsize rural Kentucky churches.
8. Hobgood, "Where There Is No Vision," p. 4.
9. An incorporated cooperative parish made up of six Disciples congregations in Bath, Clark, and Montgomery counties.
10. Tina Clarke, *Concern into Action: An Advocacy Guide for People of Faith* (Washington, D.C.: National Impact, undated), 3.

11. Lorette Picciano-Hanson, "Churches Take Role in Public Policy," *Prairie Journal*, (Summer 1991), p. 6.

Originally published in The Five Stones *(Spring 1997), pp. 7-13; used by permission.*

Chapter 28

TWELVE PLACES
THAT NEED NEW CHURCHES

Gary E. Farley

The stories of growing evangelical congregations being planted in the great cities of America have thrilled many of us who have been challenged by the magnitude of reaching the cities for Christ. We all recognize that about half of all Americans live in the 50 largest cities, and only one of four of us lives in rural, small-town, and small-city places. We support with our prayers, time, and tithes the effort to reach the cities.

Further, we hear that the vast majority of our churches are in the rural areas. I fear, however, that these facts may lead some to an erroneous conclusion: that the work of planting churches in town and country places is complete.

Not so. Thousands of new churches will need to be formed in rural and small-town communities. Based on my research across the nation, I have identified 12 types of places in nonmetropolitan America that need new churches. Many mission-minded churches will find examples of one or more of these types near at hand.

URBAN CHURCHES IN RURAL AREAS

A generation ago it seemed Americans had to make a choice to be either a rural or an urban person, with all the cultural and lifestyle implications this implied. Today, increasing numbers of us will live parts of our lives in cities, parts in towns, and parts in open country. In retrospect, it seems the challenge of the 1950s was to form rural-type congregations in the cities and their suburbs for the young families streaming from the farm, mill, and mine to the factory and the office. Today we are confronted with the challenge of forming urban-type churches in essentially rural settings.

1. *Intentional Retirement Communities*. Tim Reddin pastors a young church in Hot Springs Village, Arkansas. Its growing membership is comprised of bright, talented, affluent, retired persons. Speaking at a recent conference, Tim shared with us that this church, along with two others in similar settings, are leading Arkansas Baptists in Cooperative Program per capita support. He noted that other communities designed for active retirees are in the planning stage all across the nation.

Nearby traditional rural churches have not been successful in reaching these ex-urbanites. Barcelona Road Baptist Church has, however, so it will be starting a mission soon in another part of the village. Tim sees a need for a score or more such churches in similar communities in coming years.

2. *Recreation Settings*. Communities on lakes and streams, in the mountains, and along the oceans, many of them essentially rural in setting, are being impacted by surging population growth. The people in these places can be categorized in four ways: old settlers, newer business and service people, retirees, and fun-seekers.

John Farris, a director of Associational Missions at the Lake of the Ozarks in Missouri, has proven himself to be an effective strategist in reaching all four types. He loves the traditional rural Ozark churches and works with them to reach the local folk. He was instrumental in the formation of the Horseshoe Bend Baptist Church, which targets weekenders and retirees. He has helped some of the older rural churches near Bagnal Dam open themselves to the business people in this tourist setting. The association also operates a very effective ministry in campgrounds, other tourist facilities, and through community events. What John Farris has done needs to be duplicated more than 100 times across the nation in the recreation-based rural communities.

3. *Returnee Communities*. In the Mississippi Delta, Appalachia, and the Ozarks one meets many persons who have returned home after working in the northern and western industrial cities. Often they have difficulty fitting into the "down-home" churches, either because they have changed or the church is changed. I do not know of any church targeted for these folks alone. I do know of some that have had the wisdom to draw upon the skills of these people to make them feel at home in the church. They remain a significant unreached group in rural America.

4. *"Back to the Land"-ers.* I thought that Director of Missions Charles Kellar was teasing when he introduced me to the pastor of the You Bet Red Dog Community Baptist Church. He wasn't. The pastor, like his congregation, had burned out in San Francisco's fast-lane life. He moved to rural northern California and began drawing together a congregation of back-to-the-land folks. None came from a Southern Baptist background.

Subsequently, I met a whole cadre of pastors who had been through the hippie scene and were now pastoring their peers. What is true of the California mountains is true of similar regions across the country. Each contains pockets of very intelligent people who hold values that are biblical, even when they do not realize it, about the creation, human nature, and relationships. How beautiful are the feet of God's messenger upon the mountain (Isaiah 52:7)!

ETHNIC AND AFRICAN AMERICAN CHURCHES

Southern Baptists, as well as those in other denominations, have made great strides in aggressively forming churches with new ethnic groups and with African Americans in the past couple of decades. These denominations, and their local judicatory groups, are all expressing a deep commitment to expand work in these areas in the future. But here again, there is a tendency to rather myopically see this as a metropolitan need. Not so!

5. *African American Churches in the Rural South.* In helping associations in the rural south analyze census and church membership data, I have become convinced that the greatest need for mission work in many of these associations is among the African American population. A too-little-followed example of this work is that of Clarence Hanshew and the Savannah River Association in South Carolina. They have worked to strengthen the program of the black churches, train African American pastors, and develop a strong fellowship. In retirement, Clarence continues to work with a black church on Daufuskie Island.

6. *Ethnic Churches in Rural America.* When director of missions Tom Wenig introduced me to our pastor at Lexington, Nebraska, I met a man excited about the prospects of his church and its work in that community. A few weeks earlier a major food processor had announced that they were

coming to this town of about 5,000 with 1,200 new jobs. It is anticipated that many of the workers will be Asian. We strategized a response. In Stillwell, Oklahoma, another food processor is hiring a largely Hispanic workforce. A mission has started. There is every indication that the need for ethnic churches in rural America will expand in the coming decade.

"PLAIN-FOLK" CONGREGATIONS

Most Christians in America are just plain folk; so are their churches. This decade will furnish us with at least three areas of challenge for extending "plain-folk" churches in rural areas.

7. *Mosaic Churches in Small Towns.* A Baptist mission in Northfork, California, brings together red and yellow, black and white—all the children Mrs. Button taught me were precious in God's sight, almost a half-century ago. The story of Southern Baptist expansion in California is one of the miracles of modem missions—from just a handful to 1,500 congregations in just over half a century, from a sect to the largest Protestant denomination. Today's challenge is to move from being a denomination dominated by southern migrants to one that embraces that mosaic that I experienced at Northfork. In this, California Baptists may well lead the whole denomination. In my visits to our churches in the North and the West, I have often been impressed with the mosaic character of the congregation. Not only are the races brought together, but also status and class differences are frequently bridged. They seem to reflect the same social heterogeneity that typified New Testament churches.

8. *Second Church in Bigger Towns.* Conversely, my studies have indicated that in the Old Convention areas where a community grows to 2,500 or so and the church breaks 500 in resident membership, the mosaic quality may be lost. As this happens, a second church, one that targets blue-collar, or formerly rural, or rural yuppies, will be needed. Changing patterns of industrialization, like the placement of major auto-assembly plants in rural communities in Kentucky, Tennessee, and South Carolina, will have an impact on many small towns. Many communities in these states have gotten new industries that are suppliers for the assembly plants. Some of these will grow and experience a need for a second church.

9. *New Institutions and Industries.* The Chaplaincy Commission at the Home Mission Board sees the spread of prisons in rural areas as a possible key to church extension. By getting Baptist ministers on the staff of the institution, a person who can start a church bivocationally is put in place. A new African American Baptist church in Altoona, Pennsylvania, had just such a start.

Out along Interstate 80 across Nevada, Associational Missionary Tom Bacon sees a dozen or more micro-gold mining operations. He dreams of ministers who will work bivocationally in a mine and develop a church in the community that has grown up nearby. Many of these towns, like most boom towns in the West, will last only a decade or two. These pastors will not build big churches. They will only touch the lives of plain folks.

CONSOLIDATION / EXTENSION

Some of the most difficult and challenging areas for church extension will be in the heartland. Many rural counties in the interior of the nation are losing population. Real creativity will be called for.

10. *Consolidation.* Recently, I have visited several of our churches in the former cotton belt of the old South. Pines have replaced row crops. Pines do not take much work, so the population has declined drastically. Likewise, the churches: Membership is small and aged and few, if any, viable prospects live nearby. Realistically, the future of these churches is not bright. A few have merged, while others have consolidated in a new location.

Baptist polity makes it difficult for anyone to approach the subject of consolidation with our churches. A few directors of missions have done so with mixed results. Yet the fact remains that consolidation will occur in many areas. If it is not done with intentionality, it will just happen, often with less than desired consequences.

11. *Fields of Churches.* Noting a need, Tom Sykes of the New Church Extension department at the Home Mission Board has published a book on how to do a field of churches. Typically, this means that a pastor is serving more than one congregation. This is one way of providing pastoral leadership in sparsely settled areas. Sykes sees this as a developing means of church extension in town and country settings. A splendid example is that

of the Emory Lussi family in Medicine Bow, Wyoming. He is the only resident pastor in a town of about 600. He also works with two mission congregations about 30 miles east and west. The family has become involved in the area and ministers to the whole community.

12. *Rural Missionaries.* One summer I spent time with Lavem Inzer in Nevada and Dennis Hampton in Nebraska. Both work in ranching areas. They travel long distances and have Bible-study and Sunday-school programs in ranch homes and in rural schools almost daily. Both must work 18-hour days to minister to 600 to 700 persons. Some of their work has resulted in more traditional-type churches. But much of it will always be small-group Bible studies and special-event types of ministry. We talked about how to use the media and special events more effectively to reach and disciple persons in sparsely settled places.

The tribe of Lavem and Dennis must increase if rural America is to be reached for Christ. In our efforts to win San Francisco, let's not forget Paradise Valley, Nevada. In our efforts in San Diego, let's not neglect Coaling, California. In our concern for the millions in Chicago, let's not fail to see the hundreds in Crawford, Nebraska. In our desire to reach New York City, let's not miss Hellier, Kentucky. Where can your church be instrumental in forming a new congregation?

Originally published in The Five Stones *(Spring 1996), pp. 6-10; used by permission.*

Chapter 29

THE CHALLENGES AND OPPORTUNITIES SOCIAL MINISTRY BRINGS TO A SMALL CHURCH

Douglas Alan Walrath

To understand how to encourage social ministry in small churches we must first appreciate the basic characteristics of that unique ecclesiastical happening known as the "small" church. Using the term small to describe this kind of church is itself misleading. The uniqueness of small churches is rarely revealed by defining them according to a quantitative limit (for instance, the congregation averages fewer than 75 persons at Sunday morning worship). We gain more useful insights when we look for certain key qualities to identify a church as small.

Several qualitative dynamics identify a church as small. All the members have at least some acquaintance with all the other members. The church functions like a single cell; it is a social system with a single center, a cohesive identity. The members value relationships more than program or organization. They hold in highest regard people who act out their faith. They are more likely to refer to leaders as "workers" than as "leaders." Tradition carries more weight for most of the members than novelty. Older members, especially, are fiercely loyal and often stubborn. Most members joined and/or continue with a small church because they prefer a small church. Participants feel the church is the right size to sustain the kind of congregational lifestyle that nurtures them. A majority would drop out if the church became significantly larger. The congregation accepts and appreciates "characters" who are a source of both strength and difficulty.[1]

Most experienced participants in small churches, and nearly every pastor who prefers to minister with small congregations, can relate at least one story that illustrates each of the characteristics I have listed. As a group, small congregations compose an ecclesiastical subculture that sometimes baffles and often frustrates others. But the key to understanding how a small congregation can enter into social ministry lies in discovering how that ministry can be rooted in one or more of the qualities that shape the church's life. Consider, for example, leaders ("characters") who are at once the source of a small congregation's strength and difficulty.

One member of the small church to which I belong often challenges our pastor. Sometimes he even speaks out during the Sunday service. One Sunday the two of them were disagreeing about the need for a meeting the pastor was urging all of us to attend. The subject of the meeting was the ongoing debate over hunting moose—a matter of great controversy in our state.

"Have you read this morning's Portland paper?" Peter interrupted the pastor.

"I didn't have time; I was busy finishing my sermon," the pastor responded.

Peter continued, "Well, if you had, you would be concerned about something more important than the moose hunt!"

The congregation settled in to enjoy the exchange.

"What's that?" the pastor asked.

"They're proposing to freeze the state minimum wage. Now there's something worth talking about! Don't you think it would be more important to hold a meeting about the need to protect people than about protecting moose?"

"If we tried to have a meeting to discuss the minimum wage, nobody would come," the pastor countered.

Peter's response was quick: "If you ministers were doing your job, they would!"

"Maybe we ought to continue this conversation during the coffee hour," the pastor suggested—and was relieved when Peter agreed.

A visitor watching the interaction between Peter and our pastor might assume that Peter, in spite of his obvious concern about social issues, is mainly a source of difficulty. But we know better. While at times he tries the patience of all of us, he challenges us repeatedly to strengthen our own social ministry. Peter's outspokenness is rooted in sensitivity that not only moves him to speak up to our pastor from time to time, but to challenge the rest of us to risk in ministry.

One member of our community—I will call him "Sam" (not his real name)—carried deep psychological scars as a result of his experiences during World War II. In the years before his death he grew increasingly hostile. He became so angry at the church that he even threatened the pastor with physical harm. Though we knew him to be a lonely man and longed to extend our care, most of us were too afraid to risk a visit.

One evening we were washing the pots and pans after serving an oyster stew church supper. Noticing a pot filled with leftover oyster stew, Peter asked, "Has anyone taken some oyster stew to Sam?" Stony silence. "Put some in one of those quart containers and I'll take it to him," said Peter. We did so and handed it to him. He started up the stairs from the church basement, then paused and looked back at all of us watching him go, and said, "If you hear a shot, don't come over, just call the sheriff."

Strong personalities like Peter combine with the rest of the unique qualities common to small churches to give a distinctive shape to each small congregation's social ministry. We need to honor the key qualities that mold small churches when we want to help our own small congregation begin a social ministry.

1. *In a small congregation social ministry affects everyone, not just those who advocate it. To establish a social ministry solidly in a small congregation leaders must consider the entire congregation.* Beginning a social ministry presents strong challenges to a small congregation. Even those who don't become directly involved in the ministry, and not everybody will, feel implicated—even those who are against the ministry.

When Peggy revealed herself as an incest survivor one Sunday at St. James' Church and asked those gathered for worship to support her, her action was felt personally by every member of the congregation—even those not in attendance. The comment offered by a parish member—"We knew we would support her; she's one of ours"—catches the feeling of solidarity that is typical of small congregations.

The sense of bonding is so strong in most small churches that even those who disagree with a controversial social ministry rarely leave a small congregation. They may withdraw from activity, and, if they are really against the direction the church is taking, protest by withholding their pledge. But they rarely leave the church altogether; they are more likely to hang in and criticize. Their ongoing relationship to the church is more basic than a current program or direction the church is taking.

2. *In view of the strong bonds members feel for one another, introducing a social ministry nearly always stresses a small church. Those who introduce the ministry need to help church members respond creatively*

to the stress. In a congregation where all the members have at least some acquaintance with all the other members, whenever some new direction or concern is introduced into the church, everyone feels called upon to respond in some way. When leaders deal directly with all the members, not just those who support the new ministry, even those who disagree will most likely find they can continue to belong.

When not everyone affirms a new social ministry we advocate, it is important to give others an opportunity to appreciate why we are deeply engaged by it, and to give ourselves the opportunity to appreciate why they are not. One evening at the governing board meeting of my small church one of the members became very critical of our pastor. She berated him for the amount of time he was spending in the housing ministry, which is a central social ministry of our small church. She suggested that his time could be better spent visiting church members.

The pastor stopped the order of business. He recognized that her issue was not the amount of time he devoted to the housing ministry, but the fact that he (along with some of the rest of us) was involved in it at all. Firmly, but gently, he explained that he engages in social ministry because "it is my calling. If I cannot fulfill that calling in this congregation, then I will need to find a congregation where I can fulfill it." The board as a whole then spent a considerable length of time discussing the church's commitment to the housing ministry and the pastor's role. In the end they reaffirmed the housing ministry and the pastor's role in that ministry. They also affirmed the different perspective of some who are not active supporters of this social ministry. The *open discussion* of viewpoints and recognition that there are different viewpoints concerning the ministry helped to affirm both those who are and those who are not in favor of the ministry.

Those we interviewed at St. James' who are not strong supporters of the parish's ministry to incest survivors feel similarly recognized and included. The priest and others who are involved directly in the social ministry have worked hard to include all parish members in the ministry. Priest and congregation affirm those who do and those who do not want to be directly involved.

The strong sense of community that is characteristic of small churches encourages members to be loyal to one another and to the church, even in times of stress. Wise leaders do not discount the loyalty of members who disagree with them.

3. *When a small church engages in substantial social ministry, the church is likely to become identified locally by that ministry. The church will then be challenged to live up to its new identity.* St. James' is no longer identified in its area simply as an Episcopal church, but as the church that accepts and ministers to survivors of incest and other forms of family violence.

St. James' has already been challenged to grow according to its new reputation. One result is a center dedicated to helping victims of family violence become survivors. The center came into being both in response to the congregation's sense of calling and the community's challenging the church to live up to its reputation. St. James' self-image and its reputation have been drastically altered; it is no longer free to be an ordinary small church.

Leaders of another small downtown church discovered the challenges social ministry brings as they support their pastor in his struggle with alcoholism. Recognizing the important help he received from Alcoholics Anonymous, the church became host to several AA groups. A growing number of recovering alcoholics in that town, drawing inspiration from the congregation's willingness to accept the ministry of a pastor who struggles as they do, have come to feel especially welcome in this church. However, the new participants press the congregation in unanticipated ways. They encourage the congregation to minister to their spiritual needs, not just help them cope with their alcoholism. Pastor and congregation have been challenged to identify spiritual dilemmas to which alcoholics are especially vulnerable and to discover how to help them address these dilemmas.

4. *When a small church establishes a controversial social ministry some members of its larger community will respond negatively. Pointed social action almost always engenders some criticism.* Our research at St. James' revealed that some members of the larger community are uncomfortable with a church that talks openly about incest and that openly supports survivors of family violence. Embracing a social ministry that reflects the gospel may make a church controversial. Scripture warns us that the gospel will be a stumbling block to some. It is.

The congregations that compose the parish where I am a member engender a surprising amount of criticism with a social ministry that on the surface appears much less controversial than St. James' social ministry. We build or repair houses for those who are poor or victims of disasters. What could be controversial about that?

One Thanksgiving eve a house located about one-half mile from our church and occupied by a family of very limited means burned to the ground. Our pastor was on the scene early the next morning to help them find temporary housing. The church coordinated efforts to gather clothing and other basic furnishings. But when neighbors learned from the volunteers who cleaned up the debris left from the fire that the church intended to help this family rebuild their house, some of the neighbors became angry. They did not want this family of modest means whose yard contains some "parts" cars (called "junk" cars by the more affluent) back in their neighborhood.

Our social ministry encountered even more violent community reactions when we repaired homes belonging to active alcoholics, unemployed persons, and especially the home of a woman reputed to be a prostitute. Like the members of St. James' Church we have discovered just how domesticated the church is in American society, and how scandalous congregations become when they challenge social convention.

5. *When a small congregation becomes identified by its social ministry, that identity limits or[to put it positively] focuses its appeal.* A small congregation that becomes a social-activist church discovers that it has more appeal to some, and less appeal to others.

As I suggested at the beginning of this article, the strength of small churches is often most evident in what they do. When it comes to social issues especially, members of small churches are more likely to be "doers" than "talkers." In fact, people who simply like to talk about issues may be uncomfortable in a small church that expects members to act out their social concern.

I recall the visit of one such person to our small church. He had moved to the area to assume an important administrative position. In the community where he lived previously he had been a member of a large congregation of the same denomination as ours. After the service during the coffee hour he asked one of our members whether we have any "groups that discuss social issues." She replied that we don't have such groups.

"Aren't you concerned about social issues?" he wondered.

"Oh, yes," the member responded.

"How do you express that concern?"

"We have a housing ministry," she told him. "We help build houses for people who have lost theirs in fires or who are poor or handicapped or for some other reason are unable to build or repair their own houses.

Would you like to help us? We have a work group that will be working on a house all this week."

The direct invitation seemed to make him quite uncomfortable. "He couldn't help this week," he said. "Perhaps another time?" "Perhaps," he said. He has never come back to our church.

When a small congregation's life is centered around social action, new people who are attracted are more likely to be people of action. One woman who is a recovering alcoholic and who has become a member of the downtown congregation that focuses its social action in ministry to alcoholics told me that she assumed joining the church included becoming active in its ministries. Such is often the case with those who join a small church through its social ministry. And usually their life experiences equip them well for ministry. The woman who is a recovering alcoholic now works in the youth ministry of her small church. By grace her past struggles strengthen her current ministry. "Those young people know they can't fool with me," she said, as we talked about her work. "I know when they're on something—and I can tell them about the horrors they're risking—because I've been there. They take me seriously because they know I've been there." When a small church's reputation for social action is strong, those who join the church expect membership to include ministry.

6. Social ministry offers "victims" an opportunity to become victors. They become means of grace as they join in the ministry that was a means of grace to them.

Such is the experience of the family whose house burned that Thanksgiving eve. Throughout the winter representatives from our housing ministry worked with them to draw plans for a new house. During the summer volunteers from other churches joined with them and us to build the house. Then, on a late summer Sunday, we were heartened when they came to our worship service. Though they had never been church members, as we worked with them they had obviously become comfortable enough with us to feel they would be accepted and acceptable in our church. As the winter progressed their worship attendance became regular, and they joined in other church activities. In the late winter they asked our pastor to meet with them to tell him that they wished to be baptized and join the church. On a spring Sunday, in a sacramental celebration, as they joined with us we joined with them to give thanks together for the grace God brings to our common lives.

Those who are drawn to a small congregation in response to its Christian action are likely to want to join the action themselves. They see action as a part of membership. They want to share with others the gifts that have been given to them. Only a few months after that family joined our church a tragic flood struck the area. When the church gathered clothes and furniture to give to families whose homes were swept away, those new members whose home we helped rebuild were in the forefront of the volunteers. Having received grace themselves they are moved to pass it on.

Few small churches have the need or desire to become large. The natural growth of a small church is not in members but in ministry. While small churches are nearly always ready to welcome a few more active participants, members of most small congregations don't believe they need a lot of members to be effective. Like that small group of characters who responded to Jesus' first call, contemporary disciples in small churches discover their strength as they risk ministry. They grow strong in faith as they become doers of the Word.

NOTE

1. For more discussion of these characteristics see Carl Dudley, *Making the Small Church Effective* (Nashville: Abingdon, 1978), as well as Carl Dudley and Douglas Alan Walrath, *Developing Your Church's Potential* (Valley Forge: Judson Press, 1988); Anthony G. Pappas, *Entering the World of the Small Church*, revised and expanded edition (Bethesda, Md.: The Alban Institute, 2000); David Ray, *Small Churches Are the Right Size* (New York: The Pilgrim Press, 1982); Douglas Alan Walrath, ed, *New Possibilities for Small Churches* (New York: The Pilgrim Press, 1983); Allan W. Wicker, *An Introduction to Ecological Psychology* (Monterey, Calif.: Brooks/Cole Publishing Co., 1979).

Originally published in Action Information *vol. 16, no. 5 (September/October 1990): pp. 1-5.*

Chapter 30

NEW REALITIES REQUIRE NEW RESPONSES

Anthony G. Pappas

For many years now, many other small-church yea-sayers and I have articulated the many positives of the stable culture and community of the small church. We have pointed to such things as the soul satisfaction to be found in long-term familial relationships, the power of tradition, and commitment to place as the basis of authentic ministry.

Small-church detractors have looked at the other side of that same coin. They have pointed to the glacial rate of change in many small churches, the debilitating impact of "We've never done it that way before," and the introversion often resulting from an undue emphasis on history and heritage.

I have enjoyed this debate. It has helped us to focus on the issues and values relating to small-church life and health. But I'm afraid it's all academic now. To talk about stability in the small-church congregation and stability in the environs of the small church is to be years behind the social reality our small churches are facing. As I have traveled and spoken with church leaders from Maine to Arizona, from Alaska to Georgia, I have found a remarkable similarity in the transitions that are confronting them. Independent of geography, of urban-suburban-rural distinctions, of ethnic criteria, of the extent of disposable income, churches seem to be facing a common dynamic. This force seems to be a direct result of the pervasive mobility and (at least, relative) affluence throughout our society. Its impact on congregational life has three direct manifestations, and they all are destabilizing. Mid-sized and large churches, often more accustomed to social flux, may be better equipped to deal with these dynamics. But the small church, whose strength was once found in its stability, has to look these shifts squarely in the eye and adapt! These three dynamics are *cultural multiplicity, attendance interruptus,* and *seasonal population shifts.*

THREE DYNAMICS

Cultural multiplicity refers to the nitty-gritty reality that people may be neighbors and still be worlds apart. Of course, people have always varied in personality, tastes, and values. But, heretofore, one could assume that those on the farm, in the village, and even in the cities were in each instance cut from the same cultural cloth. One could assume that and be correct a high percentage of the time. How things were done differed over regions of the country and over urban-rural gradations, but within each category the cultural consistency was remarkably high. Not so any longer. The creation of "exurbia" means that people who do things in a city way now live in the country. And they go to the little country church and in all spiritual zealousness disrupt the monolithic stability of centuries. The creation of mechanized farms and agribusiness, requiring less manpower, means that people who prefer to do things in a country way now find themselves looking for work in the city. (I read that there are now more Native Americans living in cities than on reservations!) And, even where people have stayed put, the generation born after 1945 does not think, feel, or act like its parents. For example, they make short-term commitments only (marriage or study groups, the same), are motivated more by personal benefit than by duty, guilt, or the good of the whole, and view all of reality in terms of pluralism and relativism. These folk might sit in the same pews as their parents but they are not in the same cultural universe! And in different ways, that is true of the generation born after 1964, too.

Cultural multiplicity is a fact most churches face. What they do about it varies. Sometimes the churches blink and various integrative procedures are adopted (more on this below). Sometimes they try to make reality blink. Consciously or unconsciously these churches screen newcomers for those of cultural consistency, and, consequently, minister to a smaller and smaller portion of their community.

The second destabilizing dynamic at work I call *attendance interruptus*. If cultural multiplicity means that the people in the pews are different people, *attendance interruptus* means that they are there on different Sundays. People simply do not attend their church services 52 Sundays a year anymore. Some are absent for months at a time because they live in two places, and so are seasonal residents (more on this below). But most are irregular in attendance because a new lifestyle has become the nation's norm. This lifestyle is made possible by car and airplane, treasures living for a fun-filled weekend, and defines such fun as occurring "away." When I lived on Block Island, those few of us who were there on October 1 were here for the "duration," till June! And, being there, church was a happening. Only illness or an ice storm would keep the faithful away. Today there is no duration. It is all flux. Folk are here today and gone tomorrow—shopping in Boston, being entertained in New York, or visiting in New Hampshire. Roger Ramsel told me that when he first started pastoring a Hopi Indian church on the mesas of Northern Arizona years ago, people lived a truly village life. Their world—social, economic, religious, leisure—was contained in their village. Today, though, even the poorest Hopi is liable to be in Flagstaff, Winslow, Albuquerque, or Phoenix when a weekend rolls around!

The implications for the church are significant. A core group of regulars has been replaced by a pool of participants, or, often, spectators. Communication, if oral, often must be repeated three or four Sundays running if it is to reach the majority of the congregation. Communicational grapevines have been replaced by fig leaves! The fabric of congregational fellowship has become a loose weave at best. Identification with one's "home" and concern for righteousness there is correspondingly weaker. Predictions that tomorrow's church will resemble the chapel at a large airport are undoubtedly premature, but the assumption of a continuously connected core is outdated.

The third dynamic is *seasonal population shifts*. Block Island's winter population hovers around 750, but packs in 15,000 people on a pleasant summer day! Church attendance varies, too, but not by the same proportion! The 50 to 60 who come in the winter rises to 90 to 100 in the summer. I used to think that Block Island represented a unique church situation. Maybe it still does in extent, but in the fundamental dynamic of seasonally different congregations, I now believe it is simply part of the general norm of church life. Protestant churches are graying and as retirees live longer with more disposable income, they regularly winter in the south or summer in the north. They also travel the globe for fun and travel the country for extended stays in the delightful company of cooing grandchildren. Some hop into their RVs for destinations unknown. "See you in three months," our trustee chairman bids me good-bye each year! Some alternate between their home-for-the-past and their home-for-the-future, a retirement community apartment. Working families today often have a vacation home— usually close enough to get to, but far enough away to feel free from responsibilities, including church responsibilities. Only the most desperate of

Maine's destitute, I was surprised to discover, do not have a summer "camp" somewhere back in the woods or up a river!

Like the GIs in France, these folk tend to love the church they are with, but they aren't with any one church for 12 months out of the year. Often being people of sincere Christian faith, they get involved with a church on a seasonal or occasional basis. This creates some interesting dynamics. The Block Island church aggressively recruits its seasonal attendees to a category of connection to the congregation called "Friends," then politely invites them to pledge. Their generosity is a big help fiscally, but these folks regularly say, "We wish we could give more, but supporting two churches is tough, you know." (This is, of course, quite true. After supporting the expenses on two houses how much can be left for the Lord's work?) Occasionally—once a decade or so—a feeling of guilt makes me wonder if the Friends dollars come directly out of their giving at home. I have been known to be prayed over by the deacons after such a debilitating episode.

Having a significant fraction of the congregation with a finger in two church pies can be stimulating or debilitating. Differences in perspectives and practices can sometimes energize a freshness or even renewal, but often the transferred ideas come with a negative judgment, decrease the self-esteem of the congregation, and don't fit anyway. A pastor friend once lamented about the difficulty of keeping "the New Jersey mafia" in check in his rural Vermont congregation!

But probably the most destabilizing effect of seasonal population shifts is simply the absence of key *be-ers* and *do-ers* in the life of the congregation. For some reason people don't bring a casserole to a covered-dish supper when they are 2,000 miles away, nor do they remember to get to church early to turn on the heat on a cold Rocky Mountain January Sunday if they are basking in 90-degree temperatures outside their Florida condo. Those left behind often despair, resent, or simply can't step into the shoes of those gone off. I once compounded my troubles as pastor by asking one snowbird to still be on the trustee board because two-thirds of him was better than 100 percent of whoever else I might ask. He was so flattered he quoted me all over the congregation. Luckily, they let me stay around!

These three dynamics—cultural multiplicity, *attendance interruptus*, and seasonal population shifts—are destabilizing for the life of the small church. And yet they are what most of us are facing, to one degree or another. What are some constructive responses to this recent reality?

CONSTRUCTIVE RESPONSES

Cultural multiplicity is a pervasive reality that is frequently invisible. Do you remember those old late-show movies about an invisible man who keeps rearranging the furniture, bumping into people, and otherwise generating havoc? Culture is an unseen force that is capable of generating harmonious progress when it is consistent and constructive. But when it is different and conflicting, much havoc typically results. The effects—interpersonal hostility, backbiting, dropping out, paralysis, wasted energy, congregational splits— are all too visible! The first step in a positive response to cultural multiplicity is to *make visible the invisible*—to see the differences as cultural, rather than personal or spiritual. On this informed diagnosis a quality prescription can be made. Fortunately, we currently have good-quality resources to help us understand cultural differences in the church. Carl Dudley has written on the affective versus the rigorous. Doug Walrath describes cohorts of Strivers, Choosers, and Calculators. Tex Sample unpacks three cultures, left, middle, and right. And I have painted the picture of traditional vs. modern social functioning.

Second, when congregational leaders see their challenges and tensions as cultural, a response of faithfulness can be invited. When one culture meets another four responses are possible:

1. *The newer or less powerful culture can be denied, ignored, or shut out.* This may "work" for a while, but as the newer culture gains power, the older cultural church becomes, in effect, an outpost mission. A congregation could elect to be an outpost mission. It could exult in its calling to continue to minister to the faithful remnant. It could let time and people pass it by, as it keeps its own heritage alive. I personally would not fault this decision, if it is in fact a response to God's call to that congregation. In that case joy would be present, not lament, understanding, not confusion. Unfortunately, most congregations that go this route do it ostrichlike and pay the price for their lack of vision in the discouragement of the congregation.

2. A second response is to attempt to *create a compromise culture*, taking some elements from each "camp." This is difficult to do intentionally (although it is continuously happening accidentally). Even when it can be accomplished it seldom effects a positive result as each group feels much more what they have given up than what they have gained.

3. A third response, possibly more difficult, but potentially bearing much fruit, is to *see the newcomers as opening up a new God-given chapter in the life of the church.* This approach mandates a realization of the differences between the two groups and a choosing of a middle course. A strategy to help achieve this middle course can be described as follows: different pasts, parallel present, and a common or interwoven future. (I am indebted to Doug Walrath and Harley Hunt for this formulation.)

Different pasts are acknowledged with mutual respect. Active interest, structures, and events in the life of the church that allow people to share their stories are a helpful way to get to know and respect where different people are coming from. Often more common ground than was initially assumed can be found. Disparagement of different stories is not functional, and a story-telling format will probably be the most functional for small-church people to articulate their pasts.

Parallel present acknowledges the differing needs of the two groups. For example, in my congregation I taught a somewhat traditional Bible study during a Sunday school hour that was attended almost exclusively by the "old guard." In addition I organized a midweek, late-afternoon seminar on life issues. It was issue focused and the scriptures were referenced to illuminate high-quality choices and functional relationships and lifestyles. Some of our older people didn't get it. They were politely reinvited to the Bible study. Most of the seminar attendees were new people in town and younger in age. At first the need for two groups was not understood—the wholism of a small church creates a need to know and somehow be a part of everything that is going on—but eventually each group acknowledged the other format as OK for those attending it. This acceptance is not a trivial accomplishment and much love and patience and explanation is often required to make it occur. "I'm OK, you're OK" is a much different understanding than "We're OK," and small-church people need to be nurtured into it. The compartmentalization so often a part of the newcomer's life requires less attitudinal adjustment! A *common or interwoven* future will occur as both groups make decisions and act for the benefit of the whole.

4. A fourth response to the newcomers is for the established small church to *start a mission church for the new folk.* Sounds crazy, doesn't it? Yet most denominations have a rich heritage of starting ethnic mission churches. Why is it so hard for us to see the different culture of the new folk in ethnic terms?

Responding in love and faithfulness to cultural multiplicity is, and will be for the foreseeable future, one of the church's greatest challenges. I believe that a congregation that accomplishes even a modest amount of success in this enterprise will cause much rejoicing in heaven! Persevere!

Attendance interruptus is a wearisome and frustrating reality to those of us who have experienced corporate consistency. But for that very reason it demands our attention. Again, the first positive response is to recognize reality and accept it as our starting point for ministry. Eighteen years ago on Block Island, a typical Sunday saw 50 people at worship out of, say, 55 possible active members. One recent Sunday, 50 people worshiped out of a possible pool of nearly 200. Now, I could resent the fact that after 18 years of ministry there was little or no numerical growth to show for my efforts. I could lament the reduced level of commitment. Or I could choose to rejoice that our congregation has nearly quadrupled the *breadth* of its ministry!

Second, oral, one-time communication must be supplemented with written, multiple-time communication if the message is to get through! Fourteen years ago I was present (and helping, at least so I thought) at the birth of our daughter. As soon as Becky had been spanked and cleaned and my wife settled down to rest, I called our best friends in the congregation with the news of the birth of our first-born. Their response? "Yeah, we know." How could they know? It just happened. It seems our hasty flight to the hospital had been communicated to the island nurse, who had called a friend on the hospital staff, who had run to a phone as soon as Becky had appeared, and told the island nurse who had called everyone she could think of! Today, a new baby might be two years old before "everyone" gets the word! Routinely, news is now announced orally in worship, printed in the worship bulletin for a number of Sundays, included in a short piece in the bimonthly newsletter, provided with information via a special mailing, and/or written in a piece for the local newspaper. One-time, oral is now many-time, written communication in order to achieve the same result!

And finally, we need to keep the eleventh commandment—*thou shalt be redundant*! Say it again and again in different ways to different people in different contexts if you want to get the message across. One year our stewardship chair, in addition to stewardship minutes in worship and a stewardship sermon, wrote four (count them, four) letters asking folks to pledge. He mailed one a week to whoever had not yet responded. Two people complained about the postage, but the word got out. As a result, four more families pledged, the total went up over $5,000, and the returns came back two months earlier!

Seasonal population shifts can also be turned to advantage in the congregation that seeks to creatively respond to social reality. When it became evident to our congregation that a significant portion of our church family was physically present only a certain fraction of the year, we added a way to join our church. In addition to full membership with all its rights and responsibilities, we created a category of affiliation we called "Friends of the Harbor Church."

Friendship allows seasonal folk to feel and truly be connected with the congregation, a part of the family, while they are on the island and while they are not. Friends can get involved in the church structure as much or as little as they wish. We also found a handful of year-round residents who, for historical or theological reasons, desired to be connected to our congregation but not as members. With Friendship we had a place for them. Then, in order to keep our Friends informed, we added a summer congregational meeting, which has been the occasion for some serendipitous blessings.

Second, since our people were going out anyhow, we have found a way to baptize their "off" season or their travels through short-term mission work. The congregation has helped send Barbara for a five-month ministry to the Hopis, Bill K. for three summers as director of baseball camp at the regional denominational camp, Louise to Nicaragua to teach English as a second language, Bill P. to the former Czechoslovakia to assist with the development of an environmental bank, David and Dianne to a Native American orphanage for a week of building maintenance, David signed up for another week of mission work in the Dominican Republic, and Brad and Jane are exploring a three-month ministry in Hopi, Arizona! We gained a sense of pride as we were involved through them in further ministry!

Finally, send and receive seasonal folk with Godspeed. Wish them well on their travels when they leave and welcome them warmly when they return. Every Christian is an ambassador for our God wherever they may be. Let us replace guilt, lament, and irritation with support, affirmation, and expectancy!

Yep, it's a brave new world out there. The comfortable social patterns of the past are now, in large measure, a thing of the past. Yet God still has a plan and a people even for this age. Let us be about finding God's will and getting on with doing it. If the small church needs to take on forms more like an extended family of cousins, or a loose association of clans, we can still

bring the redemptive qualities of spiritual family life and fulfilling tribal functioning into these new forms, if we respond in faithfulness.

Originally published in The Five Stones *(Winter 1997), pp. 2-7; used by permission.*

Perry Bell is former associate Conference Minister for Mission and Stewardship, Wisconsin Conference of the United Church of Christ.

John H. Bennett, D.Min. is the Director of the Missouri School of Religion Center for Rural Ministry, an institution historically related to the Christian Church (Disciples of Christ), which pursues a mission of lay ministry training and rural advocacy in an ecumenical context. For more information, see the Center for Rural Ministry's Website at www.msr-crm.org or contact: MSR Center for Rural Ministry, P.O. Box 104685, Jefferson City, MO 65110-4685.

Steven Burt, a United Methodist pastor, is an award-winning writer, storyteller, and speaker, who has written books for a variety of audiences, including, with Hazel Roper, *The Little Church That Could: Raising Small Church Esteem* (Judson Press, 2000). He started his own business, Burt Creations, to publish and sell his own books of stories, which include *A Christmas Dozen: Christmas Stories to Warm the Heart*, *Odd Lot: Stories to Chill the Heart*, and *Unk's Fiddle: Stories to Touch the Heart*. For more information contact Burt Creations at www.burtcreations.com or call 866-693-6936.

Carl S. Dudley is co-director of the Center for Social and Religious Research and professor of church and community at Hartford Seminary, Hartford, Connecticut. His numerous books include *Community Ministry: New Challenges, Proven Steps to Faith-Based Initiatives* (Alban, 2001), *Next Steps in Community Ministry: Hands-On Leadership* (Alban, 1996), and

Studying Congregations: A New Handbook (edited with Nancy T. Ammerman, Jackson W. Carroll, and William McKinney; Abingdon, 1998).

Gary E. Farley serves in a bivocational ministry as director of missions for the Pickens Baptist Association in Carrolton, Alabama, a judicatory that cooperates with the Alabama and Southern Baptist Conventions, serving 33 congregations and a Hispanic mission in rural western Alabama. He is also a co-founder and partner with the Center for Rural Church Leadership, and does consulting work with rural churches. For over 40 years he has pastored rural and small-town churches in Missouri, Tennessee, and Georgia, and has taught on topics related to rural church ministry in numerous seminaries, Bible schools, and colleges, For more information on the Pickens Baptist Association, the Center for Rural Church Leadership, as well as additional articles and resources on rural church ministry, visit these Websites: www.pickenscountyba.com; www.pickens.net/~pba/; and www.ruralchurch.org.

Lawrence W. Farris is a teacher, writer, and pastor, and is the author of *Dynamics of Small Town Ministry* (Alban, 1999). In addition to small towns, he is fascinated by inter-religious studies and was a contributor to *Irreconcilable Differences?: A Learning Resource for Jews and Christians* (Westview Press, 2001). He lives in the remarkable small town of Three Rivers, Michigan.

Richard Griffin began pastoring in 1984 in Sumner, Nebraska at the Sumner Evangelical Free Church (about which he wrote the article contained in this book). He has since served as pastor at Circle Church in Oak Park, Illinois (a Chicago suburb), and is now pastor at Good News Bible Church in Wilton, New Hampshire, where he lives with his wife and three children.

John Koessler is chairman of the Pastoral Studies Department at the Moody Bible Institute of Chicago, Illinois. Prior to joining the faculty of Moody he served for nine years as pastor of Valley Chapel, a small congregation in central Illinois. He is the author of several books and articles and serves as consulting editor for *Moody Magazine*.

Kenneth R. Marple is pastor of Austinville Union Church in Troy, Pennsylvania, a Baptist/Methodist merge. He has been in continual rural ministry for over 35 years and directs the Troy Christian Counseling Service.

Loren B. Mead is founder and president emeritus of the Alban Institute. An Episcopal priest, he currently lives in Washington, D.C., where he is a consultant, teacher, and writer on issues of congregational life. His Alban books include *The Once and Future Church* (1991) and *Financial Meltdown in the Mainline?* (1998).

Stephen Norcross is an ordained Episcopal priest in Portland, Oregon. He has been a bivocational priest since 1980. He has combined part-time parish ministry with work as computer programmer, schoolteacher, school administrator, hospital chaplain, interim minister, and author. He is currently the Chaplain and Director of Social Serving, William Temple House in Portland.

Anthony G. Pappas has served as the Area Minister for the 50 churches of the Old Colony Association of the American Baptist Churches of Massachusetts since 1995. Previously he served as pastor of the Harbor Church (First Baptist) of Block Island, Rhode Island—a quintessential small church! As editor of *The Five Stones—Small Church Newsletter*, as author of numerous books (including *Entering the World of the Small Church* [revised and expanded edition, Alban, 2000]), and as an international speaker on congregational issues, Tony advocates for small churches in many ways. He and his wife, Cindy, are the parents of two children and live in Providence, Rhode Island.

Bennett D. Poage, a long-time specialist in rural/small-church organization and development, is the past Associate Regional Minister of the Christian Church (Disciples of Christ) in Kentucky for Kentucky Appalachian Ministry. He is currently the Executive Director of the Appalachian Ministries Educational Resource Center (AMERC) in Berea, Kentucky, a rural training consortium of more than 30 seminaries, judicatories, and ecumenical organizations. For more information, see AMERC's Website at www.amerc.org.

David Ray is pastor of the First Congregational Church in San Rafael, California, and a contributing editor to *The Five Stones—Small Church Newsletter*. He is the author of numerous books on small-church ministry, including *The Big Small Church Book* (Pilgrim, 1992), *Wonderful Worship in Smaller Churches* (Pilgrim, 2000), and *The Essential Guide to Smaller Churches* (forthcoming, 2002).

Hazel Roper is an American Baptist pastor and currently that church's Member Service Representative for the Ministers and Missionaries Benefit Board for New England. She previously served as Area Minister with the American Baptist Churches of New York State, and as pastor of the Community Baptist Church of Plainfield, New Hampshire, where she received the Rosa O. Hall Award for Town and Country Ministry. She is the author, with Steven Burt, of *The Little Church That Could: Raising Small Church Esteem* (Judson Press, 2000)

Clay Smith, a United Methodist clergy for the past 27 years, has been executive director of Hinton Rural Life Center for the past 17 years. He leads consultation and training events with small-membership church leaders across the Southeastern United States. For more information on the Hinton Rural Life Center, check their Website at www.hintoncenter.org or contact Hinton Rural Life Center, PO Box 27, Hayesville, NC 28904.

Douglas Alan Walrath is Lowry Professor of Practical Theology (Emeritus) at Bangor Theological Seminary and the author or editor of eight books. He lives in Strong, Maine, where he continues to consult with those who lead and support small congregations in various denominations.

Sherry Walrath is an active leader in the Fairbanks Union Church (Presbyterian), a congregation in rural Maine. She is a certified interpreter for the deaf, and has taught American Sign Language and deaf culture at several colleges and universities.

Caroline A. Westerhoff is the Canon for Congregational Life and Ministry in the Episcopal Diocese of Atlanta. Formerly a senior consultant with the Alban Institute, she has served as assistant to the Bishop of Atlanta; visiting lecturer in religious education at The School of Theology, University of the South; and has had extensive experience as a consultant to congregations, judicatories, and national church organizations. An Episcopal laywoman and licensed preacher, she has been a regular contributor to The Liturgical Conference's Homily Service, and a faculty member at the College of Preachers at the National Cathedral in Washington, D.C. Her books include *Calling: A Song for the Baptized* (Cowley, 1994), *Good Fences: The Boundaries of Hospitality* (Cowley, 1999), *Transforming the Ordinary* (Pilgrim, forthcoming, 2002), and, with her husband, John Westerhoff, *Living Into Our Baptism and On the Threshold of God's Future.*

Melvin G. Williams is a bivocational pastor and teacher. He is chair of the English department at American International College, Springfield, Massachusetts, and interim pastor at the Congregational Church (United Church of Christ), South Hadley Falls, Massachusetts. His D.Min. is from Hartford Seminary; his Ph.D. is from the University of Massachusetts.

Subscription Information

Congregations is published six times a year by the Alban Institute and is available either by subscription or as part of an Alban membership. To subscribe, order a membership, or for more information:

- Call 1-800-486-1318, ext 230, or
- Order online at www.alban.org

The Five Stones: A Newsletter for Small Churches is published four times a year by the American Baptist Churches USA. To subscribe or for more information:

- Call Ruth Ann Glover at 1-800-ABC3USA, ext. 2454,
- E-mail ruthann.glover@abc-usa.org, or
- Order online at www.fovestonesjournal.org